AF371790

REDEEMING RELEVANCE

IN THE BOOK OF DEUTERONOMY

EXPLORATIONS IN TEXT AND MEANING

REDEEMING RELEVANCE

IN THE BOOK OF
DEUTERONOMY

EXPLORATIONS IN TEXT AND MEANING

RABBI FRANCIS NATAF

URIM PUBLICATIONS

JERUSALEM • NEW YORK

Redeeming Relevance in the Book of Deuteronomy:
Explorations in Text and Meaning
by Rabbi Francis Nataf

Copyright © 2016 by Francis Nataf

Cover illustration by Darius Gilmont
Typeset by Ariel Walden

Printed in Israel
First Edition

ISBN 978-965-524-260-7

Urim Publications, P.O. Box 52287, Jerusalem 91521 Israel

www.UrimPublications.com

Library of Congress Cataloging-in-Publication Data

Names: Nataf, Francis, author.
Title: Redeeming relevance in the book of Deuteronomy : explorations
    in text and meaning / Rabbi Francis Nataf.
Description: First edition. | Jerusalem ; New York : Urim Publications,
    [2016] | Series: Redeeming relevance
Identifiers: LCCN 2016033484 | ISBN 9789655242607 (hardback)
Subjects: LCSH: Bible. Deuteronomy–Criticism, interpretation, etc.
    | Redemption–Judaism. | BISAC: RELIGION / Judaism / Sacred
    Writings. | RELIGION / Biblical Criticism & Interpretation / Old
    Testament.
Classification: LCC BS1275.53 .N38 2016 | DDC 222/.1506–DC23
    LC record available at https://lccn.loc.gov/2016033484

In memory of our parents,

FERNAND and MIREILLE NATAF

*W*hatever success we have experienced
we owe largely to them.
They toiled on foreign shores
to gave us the best of the values and traditions
they brought from their own homes.
They believed in us
and taught us
to believe in ourselves.

May their memory be a blessing.

ANDRÉ and FRANCIS NATAF

In memory of our parents

ABRAHAM and ESTHER HERSH *z"l*
MOSHE and RIVKA ZYTELNY *z"l*

By their children
RONNY and TOBY HERSH.

In honor of RABBI FRANCIS NATAF's
scholarship and creativity

NACHUM and SIVYA TWERSKY

In Honor of the

LONE SOLDIERS OF THE IDF,

who have left home to defend Israel,
justice and morality,
and to live by our Torah values.

Anonymous

CONTENTS

A NOTE TO THE READER

AS IN THE case of all series, my fourth volume in the Redeeming Relevance series will largely be read by people who have read several of the previous volumes. This is to be expected and is certainly welcome. Authors are greatly indebted to loyal readerships and I am no different.

Along with a reader's loyalty toward an author come expectations, especially within a series. The most obvious and appropriate expectation is that new volumes will be more of the same type of work they have seen and appreciated in the past. And yet, though there will be many similarities, this volume will also be different from the other three volumes because the book of *Devarim* is different from the other books that comprise the Torah.

Devarim means "words," and that is essentially what the book is about. Only one of the chapters in the previous three volumes was mostly about words; the rest were about stories. Stories draw us in and follow a more intuitive structure, such that my task was fairly easy. Stories provided the context for my observations and the structure for my analyses. Dealing primarily with words and not stories, I found this volume more difficult to write. Likewise, it will be more difficult to read.

My warning is not meant to discourage you from reading this book. On the contrary; we need to understand the Torah's words at least as much as its stories. And that has been my task in writing this book. It is my hope that the novel insights and interpretations I humbly submit will shed more light on the Torah's last book. It is also my hope that the reader will internalize the important and relevant messages that can be drawn from a rigorous study of the words that are at the center of *Devarim*.

On a practical level, you may need to read this book more slowly and pay more attention to detail. Likewise, chapters may be read selectively, starting with the topics that are of most interest. In any event, I am convinced that the serious reader will not be disappointed.

If this was a difficult book to write, it was also a difficult book to edit. On that score, I need to thank my wife, Deena, for all of her fine work in making this a much better book. So too, I want to thank the editorial team at Urim Publications and most particularly Michal Alatin and Batsheva Pomerantz, as well as it its director, Tzvi Mauer.

My heartfelt gratitude goes to the sponsors of this book, starting with my brother, André Nataf. His support and friendship over the years have been an important source of strength to me. Likewise, I would like to thank my good friends Ron and Toby Hersh, Morris and Julie Dweck, and Nachum and Sivya Twerski for their continued support of my work. An especial thank you goes to Rabbi Nathan Lopes Cardozo and Esther Peterman of the David Cardozo Academy, who have assisted in this book's production.

Finally, I want to thank the artist Darius Gilmont, not only for his outstanding work on the cover image, but also for his kind and generous demeanor, all of which make him a true *mentsch* in addition to an excellent artist.

— Francis Nataf

Moshe's Torah

M OST READERS ARE aware that the book of *Devarim* is significantly different from the other books of the Torah. For instance, words and expressions that don't appear anywhere else in the Torah suddenly appear here.[1] This is especially pronounced when we encounter a new word or phrase that describes the very same object or concept referred to by a different term in the other books. Even place names appear to be changed, such that it is not always clear whether similar sounding names (such as Kadesh and Kadesh Barnea) are referring to the same place or to two distinct places.[2]

Moreover, entire stories and commandments from the four previous books are now given completely different treatments. Moshe's new rendition of the incident of the spies that we already know from the book of *Bemidbar* (and which we will discuss in Chapter One) is the most famous. Many other stories, such as the appointment of administrative judges, and to a lesser extent the actual giving of the Torah, are recounted from a new vantage point as well.

Yet the most significant change is that Moshe generally now speaks in the first person, often telling us that "God told me . . ." as opposed to the more common narrative wherein we are told "God spoke to Moshe. . . ." The most

---

1   For example, Moshe is only now referred to as "the man of God" (33:1) or "the servant of God" (34:5). Likewise, the Jews are first referred to by the name Yeshurun (32:15; 33:4, 26).

2   See also *Devarim* 10:6, which gives us a different location for the death of Aharon than the one we read about in *Bemidbar* 20:22–29. See also Ramban's attempt to resolve this problem.

obvious reason for this is that the majority of the book of *Devarim* records a series of Moshe's speeches given to the Israelites at the end of his life, a time which, significantly, coincides with the end of their journey. We will explore whether the Jewish people's new reality is what brings about a need for a new voice and narrative style. But whatever the reason, the book of *Devarim* stands in marked opposition to the Torah's other books.

As would be expected, academic circles have attributed the anomalies of this book to its having different authorship from a different time period than most of the material in the first four books of the Torah.[3] But this is certainly not the only way to understand *Devarim*'s uniqueness. Long before academic Bible study, classical commentators looked in a different direction to deal with the issues the book raises. They studied the elements that clearly already existed in the book itself and didn't require speculation beyond that. To begin with, they examined Moshe's new and different role in the book of *Devarim*, focusing on the fact that his voice is much more pronounced in this book. Once we ourselves fully understand this undisputable fact, it will certainly be easier to explain many of the other differences as well.

For some – like Don Yitzchak Abarbanel, for example – the possibility that Moshe might have written his own words in this book presents a big problem. In Abarbanel's mind, it would compromise the book's divinity and consequently its authoritative status. For that reason, he feels compelled to push off such a notion. However, his thesis is not entirely convincing.

Other commentators feel less threatened and come to the more obvious conclusion that it is, in fact, Moshe's own words that we read in the book of *Devarim*.[4] According to this approach, God presumably made Moshe

---

3   See, for example, Moshe Weinfeld, *Deuteronomy and the Deuteronomic School* (Oxford: Clarendon, 1972), an important work in the tradition of Julius Wellhausen's documentary hypothesis. See also, however, Joshua Berman, "Histories Twice Told: Deuteronomy 1–3 and the Hittite Treaty Prologue Tradition," in *Journal of Biblical Literature* 132.2 (2013): 229–250, who critiques this approach and presents an alternative more in line with traditional sensibilities. For an overview of the classical academic consensus and Berman's impact upon it, see Aaron Koller, "Deuteronomy and the Hittite Treaties," *The Bible and Interpretation* (September 2014), http://www.bibleinterp.com/articles/2014/09/kol388003.shtml.

4   See, for example, Ramban, and especially Ohr haChaim, *Devarim* 1:1. Both base

understand that he should include his own words here, alongside the other books of the Torah.[5] But even with God's "seal of approval," the authorship is ultimately still Moshe's. For these commentators, Moshe's writing down his own words and not the actual words of God does not compromise the book's status at all. It remains just as holy and, more importantly, just as authoritative as the first four books. We will soon try to better elucidate how this can be.

The approach just introduced shares an important common denominator with the academic approach mentioned above. Both ultimately ascribe different authorship to the book of *Devarim* than that of the first four books. However, the classical commentators maintain that far from living in a different time period, the author of the book is the man most closely connected with the rest of the Torah. Still, the basic resolution is the same: different authors will use different words, and they will also see and describe events in different ways.

Chapter 1 gives an in-depth illustration of how Moshe saw things differently from the more objective, Divine rendition given in the other books. But the idea really needs no illustration. No matter how connected Moshe was to God, could we really expect him to have the same omniscience in his description of events? To have the same perfection in his choice of words? This is far from saying that Moshe erred in his word choice or descriptions. Rather, it is axiomatic that Moshe could not completely reflect the perfection – and certainly not the objectivity – of God.

All of this being the case, ascribing Mosaic authorship to the book of *Devarim* seems an effective strategy in resolving most of the issues usually raised concerning the book. The question, however, is whether such a strategy

---

themselves on the statement in *Megilla* 31b that the curses given in the book of *Devarim* (28) were from Moshe rather than from God. It is not clear from this statement whether this is the only section of *Devarim* that can be attributed to Moshe or whether it is true of most of *Devarim*. However, we find the following in the Zohar: "What we call *Mishneh Torah* (*Devarim*) was said by Moshe himself" (*Zohar, Vaetchanan* 22, p. 261a). See Shaul Regev's fairly comprehensive treatment of this issue in "Who Wrote Deuteronomy?" *Bar Ilan University Faculty Lectures on the Torah Reading*, December 1998, http://www.biu.ac.il/jh/parasha/eng/devarim/reg.html.

5   See Ran, *Megilla* 31b, who suggests that God commanded Moshe to include his own words here in the Torah.

exacts too high a price for the traditional reader. Let us therefore return to the problem that disturbed Abarbanel.

Moshe, the Man of God

Given how exacting the Jewish tradition is regarding the meaning of every word – nay, every letter – of the Torah, Abarbanel's concern is actually quite obvious: Abarbanel seems to make a connection between God's choice of words in the Torah and its complete reliability as binding truth. Therefore, if *Devarim* is essentially a record of Moshe's words and not God's, how can it have the same status as the unadulterated words of God that constitute the rest of the Torah? While this doesn't invalidate what we read in it, still, if *Devarim* is only a record of Moshe's understanding of God's commandments, surely that should make it more similar to the subsequent prophetic books than to the other books of the Torah. For what distinguishes those books from the Torah more than anything else is that they were written by and in the words of the prophets, and not as the direct word of God.[6] Why then, should *Devarim* be viewed as any different from those books?

What the above question fails to take into account is the status and level of Moshe at the end of his life and career. True, Moshe remained a human being, as will be discussed in the final chapter. Yet his understanding of God was un-paralleled, and as such, one can't really say that *Devarim* was *only* written by Moshe. Although the book would not bear the perfection of God Himself, it would be as close to perfection as was *humanly* possible.

To better appreciate the idea just mentioned, it will be helpful to under-stand the books of the Bible as comprising a spectrum of holiness. It is well known that the Writings (*Ketuvim*) are on a lower level than the Prophets (*Nevi'im*), which, in turn, are not as holy as the five books of the Torah. Perhaps it would not be a far stretch to suggest that there may be differences within each grouping as well. For example, the rabbis praise the holiness of

6   See *Mishneh Torah, Hilchot Yesodei haTorah* 7:3, 6.

Shir haShirim as something highly unusual,[7] and one could easily understand this to mean that it is more holy than the other books that comprise *Ketuvim*.

In light of this, we could say the same thing about the books of the Torah; in the same way that there is a difference between *Shir haShirim* and, for example, the book of *Ezra*, there is also a difference between the first four books of the Torah and the book of *Devarim*. However, it is not *significant* enough of a difference to take it out of the category of Torah and put it into the category of *Nevi'im*, and therefore there is no difference in its status or authority. To cite a parallel from the American government, the senator from California may be more influential and represent far more people than the senator from Delaware, but since they are both in the *category* of senators, they both get the same voting power in the Senate.

Many have echoed Abarbanel's concern that the Torah not be brought down to the human level. But we can put this issue on its head with much more interesting results: The fact that a human book can be included in the Torah is a tribute not only to Moshe but to mankind more generally. It is saying that a man can become so elevated in his consciousness and understanding that his words can be just as authoritative as the Divine writ.

When all is said and done, it is ultimately God Who allows Moshe to include his own words in the Torah, and it is He Who determines that Moshe's words have the authority of Torah. For a man to get such approval and to have his words put side by side with those of God is nothing less than mind-boggling. This is not to make a comparison between Moshe and God, since the gap between them is greater than anything than we can even imagine. It is, however, saying that with regard to the transmission of God's will to man, a human individual can understand it so well as to actually intuit it himself.

This high intuitive level was limited to Moshe alone and it is likely never to be repeated,[8] but that it was accomplished at all should forever put to rest the small-mindedness with which we limit ourselves, saying "we are only human." To be human means to be of the same species as Moshe! We have the potential,

---

7 *Yadayim* 3:5.

8 This could well be the sense of verse 34:9, which states that there never arose another prophet like Moshe.

at least in theory, to soar to the heavens and truly fathom the deepest, most profound and sublime thoughts that can possibly exist.

What Happens after the Torah?

With the conclusion of the Torah, the reader is left wondering about the future. As with all books, the Torah's words cannot stretch on infinitely, yet at the Torah's end one feels a certain loss of the Divine voice. If we can feel this as readers, we can only imagine how much more intensely those who actually experienced it must have felt.

What are we to make of this? Given the sense of loss we feel, couldn't God have continued the Torah in subsequent volumes, finding or elevating others who could become His transmitters? And if the problem is finding someone suitable, certainly God has more than one way to accomplish what He wants. It appears that in spite of His ability to do otherwise, God felt it appropriate to limit His words.

The net, and presumably desired, result of God's placing these limits is that it has provided a greater role for man. In one of my previous volumes, I mentioned the Midrash that says Moshe felt it was more appropriate for angels than for man to transmit the word of God.[9] Not only was this the operating norm up until then, it is likely the default position. That God chose to do otherwise and involve man is an anomaly, and far from something we can take for granted.

In this regard, the Torah serves a dual role: it transmits extremely important information, but it also brings up a man to give others the courage to participate in an endeavor in which they might have felt extremely intimidated. Had Moshe not been the first prophet to record his words, who would have had the courage to do so? Hence, had *Devarim* been like the four books preceding it, it is hard to imagine that there would have been any more volumes of the Bible. *Devarim* serves as a book of transition to subsequent works of

9   Francis Nataf, *Redeeming Relevance in the Book of Exodus* (Jerusalem: Urim Publications, 2010), pp. 38–40.

Jewish religious literature. In the absence of such a transition, other men may have been too afraid or intimidated to even endeavor to understand and interpret – let alone record – the lofty and far-removed words of God.

As I continue to record my understanding of the Divine text, I find that Moshe's special last book of the Torah provides an indispensable link for my own efforts. I feel as if I am writing as part of a tradition that in some way only begins with this last book.

Moshe is our teacher not only because of the information he taught, but for the information that he *created*. Without discounting the chasm between ourselves and this completely unique religious giant, Moshe shows us that God wants human beings to be involved in Torah and to use all of our creative and spiritual faculties in doing so. It goes without saying that this requires a great deal of care and trepidation, even more than the care we take with the most precious of commodities. Yet it is important for us to forever remember that our great awe for the Torah does not, and should not, preclude our involvement in its interpretation.

In the same way as the Torah was not complete without Moshe's book, the expansive corpus of Torah will not be complete without its last student's "book." It is the job of all who are able, to continue it. In this we can only echo the words of the rabbis who remind us that while it is not up to us to complete the task, neither are we free to desist from it.[10]

10 *Avot* 2:16.

CHAPTER 1

Moshe's Obsession with the Spies

W E HAVE ALREADY discussed some of the many differences between *Devarim* and the books that come before it. We have pointed out that Moshe's rendition here of some of the stories that took place in the first four books of the Torah will be different. But there is one story whose two versions are so markedly dissimilar that it requires its own separate treatment. In the first version, the Torah clearly states that Moshe is not allowed to take the Jews into the Land of Israel due to his lack of leadership while procuring water from a boulder[1] – and yet at the beginning of *Devarim* Moshe tells us otherwise.

In the middle of his recounting the spy incident, Moshe tells the Jewish people: "God got angry also with me for your sake, saying: 'You too will not go [over the Jordan].'"[2] While some commentators suggest that Moshe was not trying to say that God got angry with him over the spy incident, as He did with the rest of the Jewish people,[3] this doesn't appear to be the straightforward reading of the text. More in line with its plain meaning are the commentators who write that both the spy incident *as well as* the story with the boulder contributed to Moshe's punishment.[4] According to this opinion, however, we must discover what Moshe did wrong in the case of the spies and why Moshe himself identifies only this one reason for his punishment.

---

1   *Bemidbar* 20:12, 27:14; *Devarim* 32:51. The latter is an example of one of the quotes from God Himself that are scattered throughout "Moshe's book."

2   *Devarim* 1:37.

3   See, for example, Ramban, *Devarim* 1:37.

4   See, for example, Ohr HaChaim, Malbim, ibid.

We will now need to look more carefully at the narrative of the spies in *Bemidbar* as well as Moshe's recounting of it in *Devarim*. Once we do, we may well end up with a very different reading of Moshe's biography than that to which we are accustomed. The other choice, however, is to simply remain stymied, but such is not the way of Torah study. Its way is to enter with a willingness to climb higher vistas in order to find greater clarity, even if it leads us to unexpected findings.

What Happened to Moshe?

In the same way as the spy incident became a watershed event in Jewish history,[5] so too was it for Moshe. We start by noting its central place at the beginning of Moshe's very first speech in *Devarim*,[6] and we come to appreciate just how great was its impact on his consciousness when we see the extent to which he focuses on it throughout the entire book.

It is not immediately evident why Moshe cannot seem to get this incident out of his mind. On the one hand, we could say it is a simple question of association; as leader of the Jewish people, Moshe could not but be affected by this most fateful national calamity. On the other hand, Moshe's connection to the event seems to be much more personal than the first hypothesis suggests.

Beyond attributing his own punishment to it, Moshe also reveals his own agreement with the expedition. This in itself is somewhat shocking, as there is no hint to it in the story's original rendition in *Bemidbar*.[7] Moreover, he makes this story the heart of his recounting the Jewish people's journey through the desert. This arouses our suspicion that there is much more to Moshe's treatment of the story than we previously thought, and that the text may be revealing only the tip of the iceberg. We are forced to reevaluate the weightiness of the story, but it is never clearly laid out for us why. This is where our challenge begins.

5   See Francis Nataf, *Redeeming Relevance in the Book of Numbers* (Jerusalem: Urim Publications, 2014), Chapter Two.
6   *Devarim* 1:22–26.
7   Ibid., 1:23.

To understand why Moshe believed that the incident of the spies caused him to lose the privilege of crossing the Jordan, we will start back with the original narration of the story. Compared with other tragic incidents in which Moshe was involved, we note how unusual this debacle was in his role as leader. In spite of previous major setbacks, including the incident of the golden calf, this is the first time Moshe is rendered speechless or, in the words of Abarbanel, "his tongue cleaved to his jaw."[8] This man who was larger than life simply watches events unfold without taking any true action, so much so that it brings Calev and Yehoshua to tear their clothes in mourning. There was ample reason for them to show their displeasure both earlier and later in the incident, yet it is only when Moshe and Aharon respond with apparent impotence by falling on their faces (which we will explain below) that the two new junior leaders rip their garments. In light of Moshe's silence and prostration, it is as if he is simply not there. But why? What is holding him back?

Moshe didn't necessarily speak to the Israelites with the arrival of every new crisis, but he always took some forceful course of action. Furthermore, the incident of the spies is the first time that someone else comes into the breech, presumably in place of Moshe. When the spies bring back their negative report, it is Calev, the scout from the tribe of Yehudah, and not Moshe who argues with them. As the incident progresses, Calev's partner, Yehoshua, joins the fray as well. But not Moshe; he remains silent. Different explanations are given for Moshe's silence,[9] but there is no denying Moshe's lack of leadership in the incident. And once their leader was basically out of the picture – neither showing the way nor endorsing the words of his junior officers – it comes as no surprise that the Jews didn't listen to these two novice interlopers either.

---

8   *Bemidbar* 13–14, question 14.

9   Perhaps the most interesting is that of Rabbi S.D. Luzzatto, who explains that Moshe wasn't given a chance to respond due to the passionate zeal of Calev and Yehoshua, who were so strongly impacted by the sight of Moshe falling on his face. Malbim presents an almost lone voice of dissent, claiming that Moshe actually did speak up and that this is recorded later in *Devarim* 1:29–31. This, however, is a difficult reading of the text in *Bemidbar*. That text is generally seen as the more objective rendering of the story, in which case it would be hard to explain why Moshe's speech was left out. See also *Tzeror haMor*, which suggests an innovative compromise: Moshe felt as if he himself was speaking when his lieutenants spoke for him.

But it is not only in relation to his flock that Moshe behaves so atypically. His connection to God seems to be similarly affected. Instead of the usual crying out in prayer, Moshe relates to God in a new way – by falling on his face.

There are many ways to understand Moshe's falling on his face. One way is to take it as an expression of prayer,[10] which of course is a perfectly legitimate strategy and one which Moshe had used in the past (although he was always upright when he did so).[11] Yet until the incident of the spies, the only other time a figure fell on his face was to show God a state of particular helplessness.[12]

Helplessness is somewhat intuitively symbolized by the lowering to the ground of a person's face, that one part of the body that can readily represent a person's essence. Moreover, Moshe's prayer, if it was that, was not a request for Divine intervention: As opposed to other supplications, prayers that come with falling on one's face are generally wordless. In the one case when Avraham's falling on his face is accompanied by words – when he hears that Sarah is to give birth – the Torah tells us that he was speaking to himself.[13] And certainly in contrast to his earlier, upright prayers, where Moshe does ask for Divine intervention, when Moshe falls on his face here we read of no communication from him to God.

Another way to understand falling on the face is as an expression of mourning. For instance, when Yehoshua falls on his face after being informed of the collective punishment that came as a result of Achan's violating the prohibition against looting, it is a sign of anguish akin to mourning.[14] It is not unreasonable to understand it this way with regard to Moshe as well,[15]

10 See Myer I. Gruber, *Aspects of Nonverbal Communication in the Ancient Near East* (Rome: Biblical Institute Press, 1980), pp. 463–466, who points out that falling on one's face can well be an expression of supplication, in spite of its always being used as an expression of mourning in Akkadian.

11 As, for example, when the Jews initially complained about water (*Shemot* 15:25) and when they did so a second time at Refidim (ibid., 17:4).

12 I.e., Avraham. See *Bereshit* 17:3, 17.

13 Ibid., 17:17.

14 *Yehoshua* 7:6. Given that sitting on the ground is clearly associated with mourning, it is not unreasonable to say falling on one's face to the ground can express this as well. At the same time, in light of *Bereshit* 17:7, it is clearly not always the case. Hence the only question would be whether it is a sign of mourning here.

15 Ramban, Abarbanel, *Bemidbar* 14:5; *Da'at Mikra, Yehoshua* 7:6.

for there is certainly what to mourn. Yet the Talmud wonders[16] why Moshe responds by falling on his face; why does he not tear his clothes, like Yehoshua and Calev? Additionally, given that Moshe's action was "in front of the whole community of the congregation of the children of Israel," why was there no popular reaction to it? If Moshe was trying to censure them with his public mourning, why did they just let it go? Why did they not rebel further or, alternatively, acquiesce and surrender to Moshe's protest?

A third direction focuses more on what we just mentioned, the reaction of the people. Some commentators, among them Ramban, notice that Moshe's falling on his face was not described as being in front of God but rather in front of the Jewish people who, as we have stated, seemed unmoved by it. Ramban explains that Moshe is trying to get them to change course and repent.[17] While Ramban continues to point out that there are many other occurrences of falling on one's face in the Bible that are expressions of pleas, Moshe's gesture has little in common with them. Yet, if we see it as part of an ultimately political proceeding that is taking place here, such a reading may fit more easily.

Such an approach is developed in the explanation of Rabbi S.R. Hirsch. From the backdrop of the greater context of the story, R. Hirsch sees Moshe's bowing down as a way of giving the leadership back to the people.[18] Moshe is certainly not abdicating, as it were, out of joy, or even with any positive expectations. He simply believes that his effectiveness is at an end and, if so, there is no point in keeping the leadership for himself. This also helps to explain the behavior of his deputies, Yehoshua and Calev, who tear their clothing at such a possibility, and yet, with Moshe apparently out of the picture, have to take action themselves and try to win over the people without Moshe's help. (It is interesting to note that God does not accept Moshe's abdication either; as when He finally intervenes, He does not address the junior leaders who have just stepped in, but rather His trusted shepherd.[19])

Whatever Moshe's actions ultimately signify, his falling on the face and his

16   *Ta'anit* 14b.
17   Ramban, *Bemidbar* 14:5.
18   Rabbi S.R. Hirsch, ibid.
19   *Bemidbar* 14:10–11.

silence clearly show a new and unprecedented feeling of powerlessness. His reserved behavior here stands in marked contrast to earlier events. The essence of this weakness is Moshe not finding it within himself – neither by appealing to God, nor by rebuking the Jewish people – to get events under control.

Once Moshe falls on his face, however, his display of powerlessness ceases to be an isolated incident. His leadership style and abilities change indelibly from then on. Accordingly, when the Jews later cavort with the daughters of Moav and Midian, it is Pinchas and not Moshe who takes action.[20] And even when Korach challenges Moshe and the status quo more directly, Moshe's response is epitomized by his falling on his face once again.[21] What emerges from the incident of the spies, then, is a new, less assertive and more passive Moshe. It remains for us to discover why Moshe responded – or more precisely, did not respond – to the spies' report in the manner that he did.

Moshe's Spies

If the extent of the change that occurred in Moshe as a result of the episode of the spies is now more evident, it is still unclear why the incident affected him so deeply. For this part of the equation we will need to return to Moshe's rendition of the incident in the book of *Devarim*. There we find out that he not only agreed to the popular suggestion to scout out the land, he was directly involved in its implementation as well.[22] He was in many ways the driving force behind this highly disastrous plan. True, God had also agreed to the plan, meaning that Moshe did not just go ahead with it without receiving Divine approval. Nevertheless, whereas God did not give a reason why He allowed the plan to proceed, Moshe's agreement was expressly because "it found favor in his eyes."[23]

We cannot be sure why Moshe liked the plan, but his agreement does fit

---

20 Ibid., 25:1–9.
21 Ibid., 15:1–5.
22 Although we have some inkling of the latter already in *Bemidbar*.
23 *Devarim* 1:23.

in with a slow process of leadership decentralization and popular involvement with decision-making that we see throughout the book of *Bemidbar*.[24]

Let us now briefly focus on the general contours of Moshe's decentralization program. Moshe certainly had good reason to encourage such an idea. He would not live forever and, even if he would, once the Jews settled the land there would be a need for the local administration of the scattered settlements. Such communities would not be able to afford waiting for their concerns to reach the central government and for the decisions to come back.[25] Yet, as we will discuss later, there is a delicate balance between including the people in their own leadership and allowing them to make decisions for which they are not qualified.

It is easy to understand Moshe's overly optimistic interpretation of the request to send the spies. After setting his decentralization project into motion with Yitro's suggestion to appoint deputies,[26] he saw the people responding in appropriate ways. One example is the respectful and felicitous petition made by those excluded from participation in the Pesach sacrifice to find an alternative way to bring their sacrifice.[27] This petition was the first appropriate bottom-up amendment to the order of things in the desert regime, and it would be followed by other similar episodes.[28] Also included in this trajectory is the more complicated, yet highly significant, Divine "concession" to allow Moshe to give of his spirit to seventy leaders,[29] which we will discuss later.

Popular involvement is launched in the book of *Shemot*, when Yitro advises Moshe to appoint others to help with the administration of the Jewish nation. Moshe discusses this early on in *Devarim*, before he talks about the incident with the spies.[30] The fact that decentralization starts with Yitro could also be the key to understanding something quite puzzling.

Not only does Moshe describe Yitro's plan in the book of *Devarim* before

---

24 See *Redeeming Relevance in Numbers*, pp. 112–120.

25 See Malbim, *Devarim* 1:8, who makes this point as well.

26 *Shemot* 18:13–26.

27 *Bemidbar* 9:6–13.

28 See *Redeeming Relevance in Numbers*, pp. 112–120.

29 *Bemidbar* 11:14–16.

30 *Devarim* 1:9–17.

he discusses the spy incident, it is the *only* event besides that of the spies that Moshe focuses on, while ostensibly reviewing the whole sojourn in the desert.[31] Why does he mention only these two events? If we understand them as unique milestones in one trajectory, their being grouped together makes a great deal of sense. Both highlight the diffusion of leadership away from Moshe to the periphery, one marking the auspicious beginning of this trajectory and the other its near failure.

There is another important reason to connect the appointment of local officials with the spy story. It is not for naught that Moshe couches specifically these two events in the language of consensus. Moshe tells us in the book of *Devarim* that he approached the people with the plan to add deputies and they formally agreed to it.[32] The language he uses here is strikingly similar to the consent he gives to the people with regard to sending the spies.[33] In the first story, Moshe is highlighting his willingness to get the Jews involved in controlling their own destiny, as besides appointing others to govern under him, he first gets popular approval in order to do so.[34] In the case of the spies, however, the order is reversed. There, the initiative comes from the people – the Torah highlights the popular nature of the request by noting that it is coming from *all* of the people[35] – and this time it is Moshe who registers his agreement to the plan.

Hence the decentralization plan has reached its logical conclusion with the spies; the apprentices are now able to initiate and register the master's

31 See Ramban, *Devarim* 1:9. He is followed by several other commentators who understand the appointment of officers as a most important condition for the Jews' entering the Land of Israel, and which is spoiled only by the incident of the spies which Moshe is about to recount. See also Rabbi S.D. Luzzatto, on ibid., who connects the stories by saying the people should not have requested that Moshe send out spies, seeing that he had already been willing to take care of all their needs even when that meant appointing others to take positions of authority.

32 *Devarim* 1:14.

33 Ibid., 1:23.

34 Here we follow the approach of Rashi on *Devarim* 1:13, however Netziv and Malbim disagree with Rashi. They both comment on *Devarim* 1:13–14 that Moshe is actually suggesting that the people select their own leaders, an offer which the people subsequently decline.

35 Ibid., 1:22.

approval. Yet it is also possible that the reversal of who is petitioning whom indicates that the process went too far. At the very least, Moshe should have been wary of something coming from "all of the people."[36] Still – as we see with the men disqualified from participating in the Paschal sacrifice,[37] with the daughters of Tzelofchad[38] and with other events in the wilderness – Moshe had successfully made room for the people to approach him with suggestions.[39]

The Bubble Bursts

On the face of it, the request for spies to scout out the land was not radically different from other events that had come before it. In fact, it could have represented a welcome step forward, with even more people taking responsibility for their own future. And, as opposed to the demands of Korach and

36 Perhaps this is what the rabbis are referring to when they point out the disorderly and undisciplined manner of the people's approach (*Sifrei, Devarim* 1:22). See also Rabbi Zvi Grumet's insightful treatment of how this is highlighted by its contrast to the appointment of the administrative leaders, in *Moses and the Path to Leadership* (Jerusalem: Urim Publications, 2014), pp. 197–200.

37 *Bemidbar* 9:6–14.

38 Ibid., 27:1–11.

39 See *Redeeming Relevance in Numbers*, pp. 112–120. Our approach can also explain why in Moshe's version of the Yitro story and the spy incident in the book of *Devarim*, he almost surgically removes the other key players. His rendition of the events is initially quite surprising. We recognize the stories but the names are changed. In the place of Yitro, Calev and Yehoshua, Moshe inserts himself. The attentive reader will wonder why Moshe attributes the actions of others to himself. In line with what we have discovered, however, the decentralization process would be Moshe's legacy to the Jewish people. Realizing that the project had to succeed, Moshe put a great deal of himself into it. It was a project completely in line with his personal modesty and his very characteristic wish that all Jews become prophets (*Bemidbar* 11:29). But sometimes pushing oneself to the side requires taking an even larger role, at least temporarily. Given the Israelites' long period of servitude in Egypt, convincing them to take a part in their own governance required a great deal of activism on Moshe's part. And there may not have been any other way to get them to accept Moshe's move away from leadership except for it to counterintuitively come from their supreme leader himself. Hence Moshe usurps the role of others where they represented the process that he needed to own.

his group,[40] there is every indication in the text that this request was made respectfully. If for no other reason, it is something that Moshe tells us was good in his eyes.

Unfortunately, however, Moshe's optimism was premature, to say the least. If he hadn't yet realized that the decentralization process needed to be gradual (and perhaps never quite complete, in the utopian sense that Korach ostensibly tried to actualize), the spy incident certainly shook him out of any illusions.

The scouting mission turned out to be completely different from Moshe's aspirations for it. The spies exploited Moshe's plan in order to foil his overarching goal of bringing the Jews into the Land of Israel. Had he been aware of this, there is no way he would have agreed to the mission, let alone aided and encouraged it. But focused as he was on preparing the Jews for the proper administration of the land, he failed to see that they were not yet won over to inhabiting it altogether. Hence, he blissfully allowed the scouting mission to become a link in the otherwise worthy decentralization process he had made his own.

Given that Moshe could not but admit ownership of the plan, he had to shudder at how it unfolded before his very eyes: The report was not what he had expected and the reaction of the people even worse. One can easily imagine his shock and disorientation at what he saw. And then suddenly . . . Moshe has no words as he realizes that he completely misjudged the very people he was meant to shape. Clearly, he knew that they were capable of backsliding, but he did not realize to what extent the central plan to conquer the Land of Israel had never completely taken root among the people. On some level it was now evident that *Moshe had literally made the mistake of his life*.

Moshe becomes distraught in a completely new way. He is paralyzed by the realization of just how far he had overshot the mark. The whole project was unraveling completely out of his control, for he could not possibly direct the people whom he suddenly realized he did not really understand. As a result, and despite his good intentions, the incident threatened to undo everything

40 Ibid., 16:1–14.

that Moshe had built. (Later, we will see that what he was trying to build may have been actually much greater than what we have presented thus far.)

From what we have seen, then, it would appear that for Moshe, the spy debacle represented a tragic failure *on his part* – even more than it represented a failure on the part of his people. Accordingly, we can now understand his overwhelming feeling of responsibility. Still, questions remain. For one, in what way does Moshe's sense of responsibility turn into an understanding that it is his role in the story that, like the rest of the Jews at the time of the spies, prevents him from crossing into the Land of Israel?

The Symptom and the Cause

Netziv's explanation of how the spy incident contributed to Moshe's exclusion from the Land of Israel is among the most helpful. He writes that the process that ultimately led to Moshe's failure at the boulder began with the spies.[41] For Netziv, this process centered around the need for radical diminution of Divine involvement in the lives of the Jewish people in the desert.[42] Moshe had wanted to maintain a strong Divine presence, as embodied by the unusual providence the children of Israel had experienced since leaving Egypt. However, this required an extremely high level of moral and religious discipline on the part of the Jews, the absence of which would lead to immediate punishment.

After several related mishaps,[43] it became clear that the Jews needed to forego the intensity of God's immediate presence. Instead, they would need to accustom themselves to a more hidden level of Divine favor in conquering the land. The first actualization of this was the sending of the spies.

Netziv writes that starting with the spies' mission, the desert experience was to be the training ground for adjusting to this new modality. Although

---

41 *Ha'amek Davar*, Devarim 1:37.

42 Ibid., *Bemidbar* 20:8–12.

43 See *Bemidbar* 11:1–22, which begins with a vague description of complaints. This in turn brings Divine wrath, which destroys part of the camp, only to be followed by still more complaints from the Israelites.

Moshe accepted God's decision to lower the intensity of His presence, dealing with the change would prove to be an existential struggle for the rest of his life. The scene at the boulder is the final chapter: Moshe is given one last chance to overcome his inability to adjust to what the Jews needed from their leader, which Netziv tells us was for Moshe to definitively teach the Jews how to earn God's favor in more conventional ways. This included a more communal and subtle type of prayer than the dramatic petitions of Moshe that they were used to. At the boulder, then, Moshe needed to motivate and teach the people to pray.[44] But it was not to be. Moshe demonstrated once and for all that he could not be the one to lead the Jews into the Promised Land.

According to Netziv, Moshe correctly understood his punishment. He failed to make the transition to the hidden mode of Divine providence, which was what God had decided the Jews now needed, even if it would come at the expense of their faithful leader. Their sins led them to need the spies and it would remain to be seen whether Moshe might somehow miraculously pull off working with the transition that the spies represented. But he did not. From that point on, his fate was (almost) sealed. We can now appreciate Moshe's claim that he was punished *for the sake of [the Jewish people]*"[45] as a result of [the process that started with] the spy incident.

Would They Were All Prophets!

Netziv's approach allows us to reflect on the nature of Moshe's leadership more broadly. Moshe was ideally suited to the role of an intermediary between God's highly immanent presence on the one hand and a nation capable of standing at Mount Sinai on the other. But he was not so well suited to leadership in front of a hidden God Who would not perform any new miracles for most of the time the Jews would be in the desert. With God in the

---

44 Netziv explains that a less dramatic and more personal type of prayer was common much later on, when the Jews were not privy to overt miracles. Here, however, when God's presence was still more manifest, the Jews would need to learn that communal prayer can also elicit a positive response.

45 *Devarim* 1:37.

background, so to speak, Moshe would be challenged by having to deal with the more mundane political and social grievances that would be the daily fare of a more banal existence.

Given Moshe's intense level of prophecy, it is likely that he didn't have much patience for living a "regular" human life. We are reminded of the similarly inclined Rabbi Shimon bar Yochai when he came out of a rugged and isolated multi-year interaction with God and could not understand – or even tolerate – the vacuity of mundane goings-on.[46] Moshe was likely not much different. As such, it could not have been easy to live with the attenuated consciousness of God that the Jews had been assigned after leaving Sinai.

Netziv is of the opinion that Moshe eventually acquiesces to the need for a more earthly regime and agrees to send out the spies on that basis. But did Moshe really believe that this was what *must* be done? We can imagine the tremendous ambivalence Moshe would have felt in going along with God's withdrawal from the camp. And so, perhaps he did not go along with it: If he was aware that the Jews had experienced setbacks, his decentralization project could have actually been a way to reverse the process of God's withdrawal. If so, what he sought was to infuse the people with the self-confidence and discipline needed to bring God's more regular presence back into their camp. Accordingly, not only may Moshe not have agreed to the lessening of God's presence, he might have really been seeking ways to turn it around.

This perspective sheds a different light on how to understand events. Going back to the beginning of the decentralization process, Yitro told Moshe that his being the only leader would take its toll on the Israelites as well as on Moshe.[47] Although Yitro's plan was mainly a practical issue, Moshe may well have understood it otherwise: that not only would he be prevented from reaching his *spiritual* potential, but that the Jews would be prevented from reaching theirs as well.

Moshe saw no contradiction between religious growth and public responsibility. On the contrary, he likely saw leadership as an additional channel through which to cling to God. As Yitro had pointed out, were Moshe to

---

46 *Shabbat* 33b.
47 *Shemot* 18:17–18.

be involved exclusively in leadership it would prove to be debilitating. But in combination with more explicitly spiritual pursuits, one would fruitfully complement the other. Hence, it is quite natural that he welcomed the participation of others in a leadership that he saw as part of a larger *spiritual* package. From this perspective we can understand early events in the desert journey from a different angle. For instance, when Moshe is challenged by the men who were disqualified from celebrating Pesach, he could only have welcomed their initiative, as their action came from a desire for spirituality and, as such, was exactly what Moshe wanted to see. Moreover, it gave him reason to look forward to other Jews doing the same.

The notion that Moshe had such a vision is buttressed by a curious incident recorded only a few chapters before the incident with the spies. After a series of improper complaints from the Israelites, Moshe laments that he cannot continue to lead the people by himself.[48] God responds by commanding him to share his prophetic spirit with seventy elders. Since it appears that Moshe had already appointed judges/captains over the thousands, the hundreds, etc., in accordance with Yitro's suggestion, the need for additional leaders is perplexing – all the more so since we have already heard of other Jewish leaders that could have already helped Moshe as well. These include the tribal elders we read about at the beginning of the book of *Bemidbar*[49] and those who were with Moshe in Pharaoh's court.[50] This makes it appear as if Moshe is asking to appoint leaders who already exist. Yet God responds without raising an objection, as Moshe's request is for *leaders of a different type*. Hence, He proclaims that this time those chosen will take from Moshe's prophetic spirit, such that they will be the leaders Moshe wants.

Moshe's satisfaction with God's response becomes clear when two of the elders, Eldad and Meidad, prophesy in the midst of the camp. That they do

---

48 *Bemidbar* 11:14. The expression he uses, *kaved memeni* (it is too heavy for me), is interestingly the same used by Yitro (*kaved mim'cha*) to warn Moshe what would happen if he would not appoint more judges (*Shemot* 18:18).

49 *Bemidbar* 1:4–17.

50 *Shemot* 4:29. See *Midrash Tanchuma, Beha'alotecha* 16, which posits that this first group of elders had just died as a group. This is an obvious attempt to explain the need for Moshe to choose seventy leaders when such a group already existed.

so without official sanction makes their initiative highly questionable. But, as opposed to Yehoshua's concern for the anarchy that could ensue, Moshe seems quite comfortable with the occurrence. In fact, there is something even more fundamental going on. Here Moshe actually declares what has probably been motivating him all along – that all Jews should be prophets! In other words, as God is about to lower the spiritual level of the nation, Moshe is looking to do just the opposite and raise the entire nation to the level of prophecy.

With this understanding, we are ready to reexamine the story of the spies. From Moshe's perspective, that which began with the diffusion of his spirit to the seventy elders was to continue with the diffusion of responsibility to prepare the people's entrance into their land. Far from being part of the downward adjustment to a more mundane existence, the spies were to be the next chapter in Moshe's campaign for national prophecy. Now that it had been jumpstarted by the appointment of seventy true leaders, Moshe would continue to bring more people into the spiritually charged leadership. As tribal leaders of some sort,[51] the spies seemed like the ideal candidates.

This was all shattered when the spies presented Moshe with a report he did not expect.

We now have a more profound appreciation of Moshe's shock at the events that ensued. Moshe viewed the land as holy, and scouting it a spiritually enriching experience. Had the spies gone out with that same vision, they would have seen very different things. First and foremost they would have seen God's presence. Instead they saw big fruit, strong men and fortified cities. Granted, Moshe asked them to look at the produce, the people and the habitations, but this could not have been at the center of his plan, could not have been why sending spies "found favor in his eyes." Such details were to be secondary to the main report, which he later summarizes as "good is the land that the Lord our God gives us."[52] Good in the full, spiritually charged meaning of the word – especially as it is "the land which God gives us."

Sending spies to scout out the land was meant to be a landmark of the reversal Moshe was trying to orchestrate, in order to keep God in the camp.

51 In *Bemidbar* 13:2 they are described as *nesi'im* (raised ones).
52 *Devarim* 1:25.

Instead it showed him just how far the people were from any path to redemption. Whether it made him understand that his generation had no interest in conquering the land or that they were content to live out more mundane lives, or both, the disappointment must have been excruciating. Through the fiasco of the spies, the desert Israelites sealed their fate – they would neither enter the land nor continue to enjoy the immediacy of God's presence.

Moshe's agreement to the scouting mission was a bet on the Jews getting it right. When they did not, he was left with little to look forward to. As such, he would expect nothing more than the same fate that was sealed for the generation that left Egypt. Moshe understood that the spy episode had been the gamble that forever dashed his plan to enter the land. For even if the Jews conquered the land, as they eventually did, it would be done in a mundane way that would no longer be in line with his vision. Perhaps a shadow of Moshe could go into the land this way. But the real Moshe's hopes were forever dashed with the spies' report. Therefore it was, as Moshe says, because of the spy incident that his fate was sealed.

The Failure and the Rebuke

It is clear that Moshe was not the right man to send the spies. As apparent as this is in the episode itself, it is made even more clear by the success of his more grounded successor, Yehoshua, when he later executes a successful spy mission into the Land of Israel.[53] But Moshe's failure was not really the point, as even if he had succeeded in adjusting to a more mundane approach to leadership, it would not have mitigated the immense shortcoming in that first generation of desert Jews that led to the spy debacle in the first place.

In Moshe's eyes, the Jews were capable of meriting a miraculous and highly intensive manifestation of the Divine presence. Had they realized that potential, Moshe would have crossed the Jordan and helped establish a kingdom of God on earth. Instead, the Jews would need to start near the beginning, and from there it would be necessary to go through many centuries of trials and

53 *Yehoshua* 2.

tribulations before they would be ready to create God's kingdom on earth once again.[54]

But Moshe was too great to wallow in disappointment. Upon coming to the end of his tenure, he prepares his charges for what is to come. He encourages them to reach their potential, even if it was no longer what he once had in mind. These are his parting words, and they form a large part of the book of *Devarim*.

It was not enough for Moshe to inform the Jews of their current potential; he also wanted them to remember the true ideal. For Moshe this could be nothing less than a communal state of prophecy, which the Jews had attained at Sinai. To motivate them, he stresses that death and destruction could easily happen when they settle for less.

Yet, even without destruction, the path chosen by the Jews had no room for someone of Moshe's stature (nor perhaps that of Aharon and Miriam either). Like the Talmud's Choni haMa'agel who preferred death to spiritual loneliness,[55] Moshe could not live when his sublime life's vision had been rendered irrelevant.

For their part, the Jews would be granted another chance to slowly build up to Moshe's ideal in the Land of Israel. They would have new spiritual greats. And when the exhortations of these greats would also fall on deaf ears, these new ones too would disappear, whether by death or by simple irrelevance. They too would become mute, as Moshe had become at the spy incident; and if not mute, they would be muted by those around them. As with Moshe, even if they were there, it would be as if they were not.

And yet in spite of all this, Moshe's vision would never die. Through his life and through his charge – both of which are recorded in the Torah for all eternity – his message lives on, perpetually reminding us that there is a lofty ideal we must strive to attain. Awareness of that ideal and our need to aspire to it is Moshe's legacy to us.[56]

* * *

54 See *Devarim* 31:29, where Moshe tells the Jews that he knows that they will sin.
55 *Ta'anit* 23a.
56 We will discuss this idea at greater length in Chapter Nine.

Moshe was correct in his assessment of and disappointment in the Jews of his time. But he was also wrong. He was right that God is everywhere, all of the time, and is, *ipso facto*, in complete control of everything that happens. But he was wrong in thinking most people can comfortably live with this. Since they cannot, God removes His immediate and tangible presence from our world so that people can make their mistakes and learn from them on their own, without His overarching guidance showing us the way.

Jewish tradition tells us that a highly attuned spiritual individual can choose to live in a world of heightened God-consciousness and Divine providence. Yet in light of Moshe's isolation, it is a path chosen by very few. A great challenge for those who take the higher path – or really for anyone who has attained lofty spiritual goals – is not losing sight of everybody else. Moshe understood that spirituality is not meant to be a selfish affair, and that one cannot leave the community behind. But that is easier said than done, especially by one as great as Moshe. The higher the precipice, the farther one is from those standing at the bottom. Not only do they look much smaller than they really are, but one can barely make them out at all.

Difficulty notwithstanding, a religious leader must keep his finger on the pulse of the people, even as he tries to bring them forward and have them take a more active role in their own spiritual development. Certainly, the ideal is for everyone to be prophets – but this can only be accomplished one step at a time.

CHAPTER 2

Mishneh Torah: the Repeated Torah

ONE OF THE central features of the book of *Devarim* is its frequent repetition of information already known from the first four books of the Torah. From a rabbinic perspective, the most important ramification of this concerns the repetition of specific laws. Yet, whether we are speaking about law or narrative, *Devarim's* repetition has understandably drawn a great deal of attention. The very name, Deuteronomy – which comes from the Hebrew, *Mishneh Torah* – is most commonly understood to mean the second (or repeated) law.

Although there is also much new material in the book of *Devarim*, many readers have sought to understand why certain items are chosen for repetition and others are not. The most obvious avenue is to search for an overriding theme that would fit both the repeated material as well as the laws that are given here for the first time, but which excludes all the material from the first four volumes that this book ignores. Along these lines, Rabbi S.R. Hirsch forcefully expounds the plausible theory that the laws included in *Devarim* are the ones most needed for the establishment of a thriving model society in the Land of Israel.[1] We will not go into the pros and cons of R. Hirsch's theory except to point out its intuitive appeal, given that the events in our book take place right before the Jews' entry into the land.

Our focus, however, is different from that of most other commentators.

---

1   Commentary to *Devarim* 1:3. See also Ramban's introduction to *Devarim* for a similar approach.

Whereas the vast majority tries to make sense of the repetition found in *Devarim* by focusing on content, I would like to suggest that the actual key is not content but rather form. For if the difference between the content of the first four books of the Torah and the book of *Devarim* is not always clear, the same cannot be said about its style.

Eleh haDevarim

Our approach involves returning to some basic assumptions regarding how to read the Torah in general. Many readers will already be familiar with the principle that "the Torah speaks in the language of men," meaning that the Torah purposefully uses a standard human manner of communication.[2] While a proper understanding of this principle puts us in a better position to understand the Torah more generally, it is my contention that it will be especially helpful in understanding what is going on in *Devarim*.

For starters, using the "language of men" means that the Torah cannot be read like a standard law book. Were the Torah just a common legal code, there would have been little room for repeating things, and thus any repetition we might encounter would be attributed to oversight.[3] For the goal of a law code is to store information in as organized, clear and economical a fashion as possible. In order to do so, it lists the laws and organizes them by category. By contrast, the fact that the Torah intersperses its laws with so many narratives is just one glaring indication that it is trying to accomplish something completely different.

In taking a more "human" style, the Torah recognizes that straightforward new information is not always what human communication is about. A great deal of it has more to do with communicating an emotion, meaning that it's

2   See Introduction to *Redeeming Relevance in Exodus* (pp. 15–20), where this is discussed in greater detail.

3   Obviously, sometimes, as in the *Shulchan Aruch*, a law is relevant to two different situations and is thus stated in more than one section. Still, a streamlined and ostensibly preferable system would simply refer the reader to where the law is written for the first time rather than restating all the information again.

more about *how* something is said than *what* is said. This is true of the Torah in general, although the first four books retain the general style and flavor of a written work and thus the emotions evoked are limited. Not so with the book of *Devarim*.

One of the first obstacles to understanding *Devarim* is thinking of it as a book. *Devarim* literally means "[spoken] words." Even if we might otherwise have missed the centrality of this notion, the book's orality is brought to our attention right from the start: "These are the words that Moshe *spoke*." The text clues us in to the fact that, as opposed to the other four books, *Devarim*, to its very core, is an oral work.

In light of the book's strong oral dimension, it would be no surprise to find other ways in which it is tied to orality. We have said that most understand its rabbinic name, *Mishneh Torah*, as referring to the fact that it contains laws that previously appear in the first four books. But this is not the only way that the term can be understood.

According to some commentaries,[4] it doesn't refer to the duplication of previously recounted sections of the Torah but rather to a (section of the) Torah that requires *our repetition of it* and its constant review. Whether this is a correct understanding of the term or not, everyone agrees that it is specifically in the book of *Devarim* that we find many passages that were constantly recited by the Jews throughout the ages.[5] Hence the only question is not whether the book had to be recited but rather how much of it encompassed this requirement. This approach differentiates *Devarim* quite explicitly from the other books, as the recitation and re-recitation of it defines its very essence.

The orality of *Devarim* means that it comes with its own rules. When a writer repeats himself it generally goes against the conventions of writing. But in an oral presentation the opposite holds true, as the repetition itself is a convention.[6] In our own lives we are aware that people purposefully repeat

---

4   See Netziv's introduction to *Devarim* in *Ha'amek Davar*. See also R. Menachem Liebtag, "Sefer Devarim – Introduction," at http://www.tanach.org/dvarim/dvarim/dvarintr.htm .

5   We will discuss some of these sections in Chapters Four, Seven, and Eight.

6   Repetition in the Torah can more generally be attributed to its poetic style. In fact, Netziv suggests that the Torah is actually more similar to verse than to prose (see

themselves in everyday speech. Whether it is a parent repeating important instructions to a child or a politician turning back to a catch phrase, it is even often tellingly prefaced by the words, "I repeat." When the parent or politician repeats him- or herself, the words are not meant to convey new information, as they've already been heard by the listeners. Rather, the speaker is using the words this time to convey emphasis, as if to say, "The following is so important that it bears repeating."

I suggest that the Torah is doing exactly the same here. Although it could have written "this is important" (as does Maharal, for example, in his writings) or "note this" (as does Rabbi Chaim Vital), it would have been less colloquial and, therefore, less like the "language of men." The Torah explicitly strives to be colloquial, even as it tries to echo the highly refined message of God. And this is all the more true in its most oral of books.[7]

This approach is consonant with the view that certain commandments are repeated because of their importance specifically at the time that they are reiterated, e.g., as the Jews get ready to enter their land. Still another approach, which we also see earlier in the Torah, emphasizes not the context in which a commandment is repeated but rather its own intrinsic importance.[8] The Ten Commandments, for example, carry obvious extra importance, and still would even if they had been stated only once. Nevertheless, their being repeated accentuates their importance. In other cases, however, it is only a commandment's repetition and not the commandment itself that brings this to

---

his introduction to *Ha'amek Davar*). Nevertheless, he later points out that *Devarim* is even more in the category of verse than the other four books.

7 See Meir Weiss, *The Bible from Within* (Jerusalem: Magnes Press, 1984), p. 37, note 24, where he makes a similar critique about many medieval commentators. According to Weiss, they show literary insensitivity when they write that nothing is added when prophets express themselves about the same matter in more than one way in the same verse.

8 Although rabbinic leaders have always been reticent to express this, there are some commandments that are clearly more important than others. See Maharal's *Derech Chaim*, *Avot* 2:9, as well as *Tosafot Yom Tov*, ibid., who express this quite clearly. See also Chapter Three, note 19.

our attention. One example might be the daily sacrifice,[9] as the rabbis appear to note.[10]

Of course, one could question my approach in view of how the rabbis deal with repetition in many places. There is no question that the rabbis saw repetition in the Torah as "unnecessary" information *in and of itself.* They understood repetitive passages as clues for additional, hidden meaning. This is a fundamental working assumption of rabbinic Judaism and we have no reason to question it. At the same time, it would be fair to say that the Torah can avail itself of many ways to transmit information. Repeating words verbatim is certainly one way for it to transmit oral traditions not otherwise found more explicitly in other parts of the Torah as well as to derive new laws that appear warranted. But since there are other ways it could have accomplished this, the reader is correct to look for other reasons repetition is used to present some laws and not others.

Why *Devarim*?

What necessitated the Torah to diverge from its usual manner so drastically in this book? Perhaps just as endnotes and appendices are placed in the back of books so as not to disturb the flow of the main idea, so too might colloquial style and repetitions, which don't fit well into the standard flow of the Torah's first four books, need to wait until the end. But there is something more.

In line with our introduction, we should not forget that *Devarim* is a stylistic bridge between God's direct word in the first four books of the Tanach and the human renditions of prophecy in the post-Pentateuchal works that follow. Indeed, many prophetic books are remarkable for their idiosyncratic styles, wherein the character of the prophet stands out, often simply by how he expresses himself. To the extent that *Devarim* is Moshe's prophetic book, we would also expect it to reflect Moshe's necessarily human way of speaking.

---

9   *Shemot* 29:38–41; *Bemidbar* 28:3–5. Note that this repetition actually precedes the book of *Devarim.*

10   There is an unidentified midrash citing R. Shimon ben Pazi to this effect quoted in the introduction to R. Ya'akov Ibn Chaviv's *Ein Ya'akov.*

But even this is not enough to fully justify the radical shift in presentation that occurs here.

Perhaps the answer lies in looking at *Devarim*'s situational context. Moshe's departure from the Jewish people is not merely the catalyst for giving the Jewish people last-minute instructions and a "pep talk" before entering the land. It is also his last chance to ensure the Jewish future more generally. But for that Moshe had to have a strategy.

It is certainly important for the Jews to keep all of the commandments given them by God and to be aware of the Torah's entire contents. Yet Moshe understood that when push comes to shove, there are only a limited number of things that can remain at the forefront of a person's consciousness. About to leave the stage, Moshe needed to finally formulate what those things must be. Deciding which commandments were most central to the Jewish people's identity was a momentous undertaking, with extremely serious ramifications. It required choosing which laws most needed to be protected against their being transgressed in the future.[11]

We have alluded to the fact that commentators who address the issue of repetition in the book of *Devarim* also point out that most of the laws appearing in the book are actually new, and their inclusion has to be explained as well. It seems to me that this is open to challenge. One need not necessarily find one grand theory that explains the place of both the new laws and those previously stated. Could there quite simply be two different things going on here? Laws relevant to entering the land and creating a new society were saved for the point in time where they would be most relevant. Simultaneously, there was a need to repeat laws that were already discussed in order to reinforce cardinal principles that would be relevant for all time.

Such an approach reminds me of a childhood ritual I remember quite well. When I was in middle school, the first two orders of business every morning were the Pledge of Allegiance and the daily announcements. The only thing they had in common was that they were both appropriate for the beginning of the day – but for dramatically different reasons. The Pledge was thought to be of cardinal importance, and that gave it priority. The announcements were

11   See Rav A.Y. haKohen Kook's *Guide for the Perplexed of the Generation*, Chapter 23A.

often trivial and lost their value the very next day, but they involved information that had immediate relevance and thus needed to be taken care of right away. It is quite possible that Moshe's speech contained these two elements as well: cardinal principles such as the Ten Commandments and what was learned from the failure with the spies, as well as laws immediately relevant even if not necessarily central, such as those pertaining to kings and wars. Hence, proximity does not always imply commonality.

While we have shown that different issues can be urgent for different reasons, in the process, we have also shown that what they do have in common is their urgency. Whether that urgency is limited to those about to enter the Land of Israel or whether it applies to all those engaged in the creation and maintenance of an elevated and well-functioning community is open for discussion. But at least for the former, the book of *Devarim* is, more than anything else, *a book of urgency*. From that perspective, it represents a mini-Torah – a practical summary of how to live as a religious Jew in an independent state. And it is with this in mind that we will address the various themes we will come across.

Is a Non-Verbatim Repetition Still Repetitive?

There are a few additional points with regard to repetition in the Torah. First of all, we should acknowledge the possible difference between verbatim or near verbatim repetitions, and what only appears to be repetitive but is in fact a different – and hence novel – perspective on the same idea or event. In the latter case, two different perspectives on the same story or commandment will always add new information and therefore cannot, strictly speaking, be called repetitive.

One could take the last observation to an extreme and challenge the existence of verbatim repetitions altogether. For example, even if certain verses in the first rendition of the Ten Commandments are repeated verbatim in the second rendition,[12] one could argue that the differences before and after

---

12 See *Shemot* 20:2–14; *Devarim* 5:6–18.

the static verses infuse even the repeated ones with new meaning. But such a claim would be hard to make. It is difficult to see any new meaning added from the second appearance of these verses simply based on context. Likewise, the changes in the Shabbat commandment in the second rendition of the Ten Commandments seem to have no bearing on the commandments that come before and after them. In light of this, we can only conclude that if the Torah were looking to avoid the repetition of texts that do not add any new content, it could have spared us most of these verses, or at least cut away much of their verbiage.

Near pure verbatim repetitions are actually quite rare in the Torah. Our discussions in the rest of this book, however, will assume that there is always a need to justify repetition. And so, even in the case where a verse, concept, or law is repeated without being verbatim, we still need to explain the need for a second treatment of certain things and not of others, as well as why they need to be said specifically in *Devarim*.

* * *

Far from creating distance between us and the Torah, the repetition of certain sections of *Devarim* should further connect us to it – speaking to us, as it does, on a very human level. In the last chapter of our volume on *Shemot*, we already discussed how the Torah teaches us the need for an uneven distribution of focus.[13] Our discussion here reminds us of this concept, but it also takes us elsewhere.

We live with much variety in our lives, from the food we eat to our interaction on social media. We are also surrounded by conflicting priorities from work, school and family. In short, there are many things we need to put our minds to. The more crowded our schedules and our minds become, the more we are in danger of losing perspective. This chapter illustrates the need to find concrete ways of prioritizing those things that should be most important to us. And this is exactly what the Torah does, by repeating – sometimes several times – those things that deserve a larger share of our attention.

---

13 "The Zikaron of Pesach: Productive Selectivity," in *Redeeming Relevance in Exodus*, pp. 127–136.

Curiously, in spite of the many other strategies that have been devised over the ages, repetition may still be the most effective way to make sure that we put forward what needs to be put forward. Meditation practices, such as those used by the Mussar school, use repetition to point our focus toward needed changes in our lives. By saying something over and over or by repeating a behavior on a constant basis, we not only bring it to the forefront of our attention, we also integrate it into our very personalities. It is for this reason that Rambam suggests it is better to give small amounts of charity many times over than to give one big lump sum.[14]

Focusing on that which is most important is not the same as discarding what is less central. Minor things have their place. But so do major things. And those two places are very different. The challenge that the Torah tries to help us with is how to maintain that uneven balance, even while living rich and varied lives.

14 *Commentary to the Mishna, Avot* 3:15.

CHAPTER 3

Ten Statements and Two Tablets

THERE ARE VERY few texts, if any, that have the stature of what is commonly referred to as the Ten Commandments. Considered by many to be the backbone of both Judaism and Christianity, the Ten Commandments form part of the basic warp and woof of Western society as we know it.

As several writers have recently pointed out,[1] our familiarity with the Ten Commandments often prevents us from truly analyzing the text as a whole, and from really understanding its contours and its various messages. But more than our familiarity with the text, it is our familiarity with the norms the Ten Commandments have created that is the real obstacle. Because they feel so familiar, many of us think of them as bromides only little children need to learn. The rest of us take them for granted as obvious and intuitive.

But a closer reading of the Ten Statements – as they should more correctly be called in English – shows that they are actually meant to elicit a much more specific and profound response than that to which we are accustomed. To understand this, it is first necessary to look at them as one unit. Even if we wanted to explore them one at a time, they find their place here in the book of *Devarim* as a single document. Here, in the context of Moshe's review of the most important events the children of Israel experienced during their long trek

1   See R. Yoel bin Nun, "*Aseret haDibrot, Shneim Asar Lavin,*" http://www.ybn.co.il/about-8.html; and more recently, Leon Kass, "The Ten Commandments: Why the Decalogue Matters," *Mosaic*, June 1, 2013, http://mosaicmagazine.com/essay/2013/06/the-ten-commandments/; and David Hazony, *The Ten Commandments* (New York: Scribner, 2010), pp. 3–4.

from Egypt to the Land of Israel, they are presented as the totality of what the Jewish people heard from God when they stood at Mount Sinai.

Ma'amad Har Sinai: Standing at the Mountain

Before we look at the text of the Ten Statements, it is essential that we first examine its context. In contrast to other passages in the Tanach, the Ten Statements are more about how they were said than what they said. In other words, the main point of the giving of the Ten Statements was not because of their content, much of which was already known either via the universal Noachide moral code or through other prophecies predating Sinai. In fact, tradition has it that most of the commandments were not only known but even already observed by the children of Israel. According to at least one source, even the commandment most outside of the universal rubric – the observance of Shabbat – is said to have been commanded between the time the Israelites left Egypt and when they reached Mount Sinai.[2]

A good place to start, then, is with an interesting observation made by Rashi. He points out that at Mount Sinai, God is suddenly referred to as *Elokim*, a name traditionally associated with His strict judgment and ideal truth.[3] This means, *inter alia*, that retribution for wrongdoing and sins is instantaneous. According to Jewish tradition, this name represents an approach that God generally does not implement, knowing that people cannot survive it on any sustained basis. But obviously it would never have been mentioned in the Torah had there not been times it did need to be expressed. Following Rashi's observation, the giving of the Ten Statements appears to be one of those times. At Mount Sinai, the Jews were confronted with absolute expectations which were not even minimally tempered by God's usual trait of mercy.

The absolute nature of this aspect of God is especially noticeable in the second half of the statements, starting with the commandment not to kill. R. Yoel bin Nun mentions the completely unnuanced tone of these five statements.

2   *Sanhedrin* 56b.
3   Rashi, *Shemot* 20:1.

He explains that as opposed to other negative commandments in the Torah, where we often find some explanation and/or historical context, here there are just commands.[4] Moreover, most of them contain just two words, for in front of the God of truth and justice anything more would be superfluous.

The harsh, demanding tone of the last five statements is not completely absent from the first five either. From the very beginning we are reminded that it is *our* God involved here, the God Who took us out of slavery and destruction in Egypt. What this means – and is almost explicitly stated[5] – is that the Jewish people owe God an existential debt which justifies the demand for their absolute allegiance.

Yet as informative as the tone of the Ten Statements may be, it is the setting for their transmission that informs us of their true place in the Torah. The recounting of a dramatic encounter with God – surrounded, literally, by thunder and fire – was meant to give more than a lasting impression. It was to be a gripping experience that would once and for all cement the Jews' awareness of God's power – over them and over all of mankind. Indeed, the rabbis tell us that after God's very first statement, the Jews all died from fright and needed to be resuscitated in order to hear the rest.[6] Whether the rabbis meant this to be taken literally or not, it certainly illustrates the type of terror they must have felt.

No doubt this sense of awe and fear was even more central to the experience than the actual words those standing at Mount Sinai heard. Rambam understands that the words of the first two statements – which according to the dominant tradition are the only ones heard by the Jewish people, as well as Moshe[7] – are only a concretization of that which was never actually articulated, but rather simply understood by the experience itself.[8]

When we look at *Ma'amad Har Sinai* as a whole, we see a carefully designed

---

4   See R. Yoel bin Nun, *op. cit.* See also Nahum Sarna, *Exploring Exodus: The Roots of Biblical Israel* (New York: Schocken, 1996), p. 142.
5   *Shemot* 20:2; *Devarim* 5:6.
6   *Shabbat* 88b.
7   *Horayot* 8a. According to Ramban, however, what is meant is that while all ten were heard, only the first two were understood without the mediation of Moshe.
8   *Moreh Nevuchim* 2:33.

and orchestrated production to compel unswerving loyalty to God. Both the content of the Ten Statements and their delivery make the basic message clear to anyone reading them: The Jews owe their existence to God, and therefore they must submit to His yoke. To make this perfectly clear, a few main points regarding what this entails are immediately enumerated.

Many writers familiar with the Ancient Near East have pointed out the resemblance between the Ten Statements and a suzerain's treaty with his vassals.[9] The suzerain would begin with why he deserves their obedience, follow it up with his demand for absolute obedience – predicated on the inadmissibility of loyalty to any other sovereign – and then enumerate some of the main demands he requires his vassals to fulfill.

The idea of a Divine show of power and ultimatum is precisely how the rabbis understand the revelation at Mount Sinai. They make several statements regarding this, the most famous being found in the Talmudic tractate *Shabbat*. There, God is depicted as suspending Mount Sinai in the air and telling the Jews that they have the choice to either accept His commandments or have the mountain dropped on their heads.[10] Here also, we do not need to take the story literally in order to understand that it, and other stories like it, clearly and accurately reflect the tone and substance that the Torah is trying to convey.

Why These Ten?

Now that we have a better sense of the context of the Ten Statements, we are in a better position to understand its content as well. We will begin with a key question: Why these particular statements? Why were they chosen and not others? While the centrality of most of the Ten Statements is intuitive, the reason for the inclusion of some of them (e.g., don't bear false witness, don't covet) over others (e.g., love God, love your neighbor) is not. Understanding

---

9   See *Exploring Exodus*, pp. 134 –148; R. Moshe Shamah, *Recalling the Covenant* (Jersey City: Ktav, 2011), pp. 356–360, 886–889; Joshua Berman, "God's Alliance with Man," in *Azure* (Summer 2006), pp. 79–104.

10   *Shabbat* 88a.

why specifically these ten were chosen will take us a long way toward understanding the essence of this venerable text.

One answer given is that all of the Torah's commandments are subsumed in these ten.[11] This is a clever and perhaps even plausible approach to the issue, but it lacks a strong basis in the text. Without being extremely imaginative, one would be at loss to find any indication that these ten are just a summary of a larger number. (The rabbis also do not make any assertion such as that of Hillel about what is known as the golden rule, that the rest is commentary.[12]) Moreover, in spite of R. Saadia Gaon's impressive ability to find so many straightforward connections between the Ten Commandments and their derivatives, the plausibility of this approach still stretches our credulity on more than one occasion. For example, to understand the penalties paid for damages caused by an ox under the category of Do Not Kill is far from obvious. Likewise, placing the commandment to cover the blood after slaughtering an animal under the category of Do Not Covet is difficult to understand.

Trying to fit all of the commandments into the ten, however, is not the only possible approach. If we assume the Ten Statements do not include every central precept we would expect to be included, two possibilities still remain: either we readjust our understanding of what is central in line with what is included, or we develop an alternative explanation for the inclusion of certain seemingly minor precepts instead of (perhaps, even at the expense of[13]) others that appear to be more important.

Many commentators have taken the first road, and we will not attempt to outdo the much greater minds that have traveled it.[14] Instead, we will explore the second strategy and try to explain why this great document – presented with such drama and emphasis – *deliberately* skipped over some of the Torah's most central precepts on the one hand, and included some of lesser

---

11   See *Bemidbar Rabba* 13:16. See also Rashi, *Shemot* 24:12, who also cites R. Saadia Gaon's *Azharot*, 882–942.

12   *Shabbat* 31a.

13   Since there seems to be a premium for certain round or otherwise significant numbers such as ten. After all, "The Eleven Commandments" just doesn't have the same ring!

14   Perhaps the greatest of these is that of Ramban. See his commentary to *Shemot* 20:2–13.

ultimate import on the other. First, however, an alternative explanation for the Decalogue's mixed content, and why it might be incomplete, is in order.

One area of Jewish thought and practice commonly associated with *Ma'amad Har Sinai* is connecting *Kabbalat haTorah*, the receiving of the Torah, with the notion of a mass conversion to Judaism.[15] More than one contemporary Jewish writer has written on this theme. (*Kabbalat haTorah* here refers to the hearing of the Decalogue at Mount Sinai and, through that, creating a covenant with God for the acceptance of all the laws of the Torah.) Indeed, this is the reason frequently given for the reading of the book of *Ruth* on Shavuot, the holiday associated with *Ma'amad Har Sinai*.[16] Ruth is viewed as the paradigmatic convert to Judaism, and reading about her reminds us that we also once went through something very much akin to her experience.

Exploring *Ma'amad Har Sinai* from this perspective reminds us of one of the laws of conversion: that the potential convert should be exposed to a sample set of laws that include both stringent (more central) laws as well as more lenient (less central) ones.[17] The most likely rationale for this is that the potential convert get a representative sample of that which he is taking on. If he would hear only the stringent laws, he would be misled into thinking all of Jewish practice is harsh and difficult. Knowing that some laws are less central and come with lesser penalties allows him to realize that Judaism is a doable system for the average person.[18] In line with this, we could say that the sampling given at Mount Sinai allowed the children of Israel to better appreciate

15 See, for example, Feivel Meltzer's commentary to the book of *Ruth* in *Da'at Mikra* (Jerusalem: Mossad HaRav Kook, 1973), p. 20. I have yet to find a significant reference to this in the classical literature. What comes closest is a discussion in tractate *Keritot* 9a, which derives certain aspects of conversion from the Jews' experience in the desert on their way out of Egypt. Still, even there, one finds, no mention of Mount Sinai *per se*.

16 See previous note.

17 *Yevamot* 47a. See Ramban, *Shemot* 25:1, who makes a similar comparison between the sampling of laws given to potential converts and the early laws given to the Jews, of which the Ten Statements were a subset. See also *Mishneh Torah, Hilchot Isurei Biah* 14:2, which seems to independently assert that among the information presented to the convert are ideas with a strong affinity to the Decalogue's first two statements.

18 See *Bach* on *Tur, Yoreh De'ah* 268.

the Torah's contours. Like the convert, the Israelites were made to understand that not every law has to come with a death penalty, nor must every law have to be about the underpinnings of civilization.

The above approach has its merits, although it is difficult to completely accept. For one, the vast majority of the Ten Statements *do* seem to be among the main tenets of the Jewish religion. And the others are not exactly what we would call "*kalot*" ("light," or more lenient laws).

Hence I suggest a hybrid approach whereby the Jews were in fact presented with a sampling of laws, but it consisted only of ones that were central to Judaism. There were, in fact, other essential laws that God chose not to give at this time. Although intuitive, this approach still does not completely explain the Decalogue's composition. For even if God had reasons to limit Himself to the number ten, or simply to a compact subset of central laws — as well as some that were not so central — we would still expect those presented on this auspicious occasion to somehow be the most important according to at least one set of criteria.[19] But now we are back to our original quandary. We promised to leave such an approach to others, and for good reason – it seems a well-nigh impossible task.

Perhaps the best answer is to remind ourselves that there is much more to this text than its content. The Torah's primary function at *Ma'amad Har Sinai* was to create an experiential initiation of absolute loyalty to God. Part of that ceremony involved a certain text, in the same way as a national hymn might accompany a similar ceremony upon induction into a nation's army. But such a text plays only one part in such a ceremony, and not necessarily the most important part.

In the context of an induction into God's service, certain commandments

---

19 See Chapter Two, note 8. We are assuming that it is possible to differentiate between the levels of importance of various precepts, an assumption generally accepted by the rabbis even if there are some statements in the Talmud and later commentaries that can be understood otherwise. See, for example, Abarbanel, *Rosh Amanah* 23, where he attacks Rambam's articulation of the Thirteen Principles of Faith. According to Abarbanel, there is ultimately no such thing as a principle, a precept or a religious position which can be elevated above any other. His position notwithstanding, normative Jewish law constantly prioritizes one law over another, thereby making a judgment as to its relative importance.

would be more to the point than others, even if they are not so central outside of this context. One possibility is that God would want to specifically enumerate the commandments most difficult *to commit to* (though not necessarily the most difficult, as we will illustrate). As this induction represents a ceremony of loyalty, God would want to hear that the Jews will not later seek to escape those things that – for a variety of reasons – might make them feel uncomfortable

The selection of the laws in the Decalogue, then, was determined by its context. Had they not been presented at this critical juncture in the relationship when the Jews couldn't say "no," God could not have secured acceptance of certain laws that might otherwise have been sticking points. True, the Jews would transgress these laws in the future, but that wasn't the point. The point was to give the children of Israel absolute clarity of the *nature* of their servitude to God. To effect this, the Torah needed to present them with those laws and concepts which people would most want to rationalize away with the "yes buts" so familiar to parents and teachers.

To be sure, the degree of difficulty in committing to the Ten Commandments is measured differently for each one. For example, the Talmud articulates the constant tension involved in honoring one's parents. It points out the massive challenge created by the need to completely fulfill what is required when the amount or nature of a parent's needs inevitably exceed the child's time or inclination.

Another example: Although refraining from murder is fairly routine for most people, the difficulty here is not in the required discipline. It is in the acceptance of the *complete* sanctity of the other that comes with this demand. The Torah wants to make clear that the prohibition against murder is not just a good idea in the Hobbesian sense of political self-interest. Rather, the power over life and death is something the individual must completely and totally relinquish to God.

Of course, it is possible to challenge this theory as well. What about the difficulty of the laws of physical separation between husband and wife? What about the laws of the sabbatical year, which because of their difficulty the Torah goes out of its way to encourage fulfilling? One answer is that the Torah is looking only at precepts that are constantly germane, or in modern parlance, applicable 24/7. The rabbinic understanding of the precept to remember the Shabbat as applying to all seven days of the week, as well as their formulation of honoring parents even after they are dead, bolsters such a distinction.

Questions as to why these specific commandments were the ones included in the Decalogue will always remain, but putting them in the context of a document of allegiance at least partially mitigates the issue. The bottom line is not what is most central to the Jewish religion but rather what best exemplifies the Jewish people's total subordination to God.

Two Tablets

We have so far presented God's voice in the Ten Statements as that of a strict and unyielding sovereign. Yet the Ten Statements also reveal a completely different, less obvious side of God. This is partially hinted at by the very existence of *two* tablets containing the Decalogue. Indeed, the fact that Moshe was given two tablets by the One and universal God should not be overlooked.

For the purposes of this discussion, we will divide the Ten Statements as they are commonly divided, following the more popular rabbinic opinion that each tablet contained five statements.[20] The other traditional approach is that all the statements were written on each of the tablets, so as to create two copies of the same document – a practice quite common in business and other agreements up until today. (While not considered as a third approach, the breaks [*parashiyot*] in the Masoretic text give us another possible demarcation, wherein the first half is separated from the second by a full break after the third statement, that of not taking God's name in vain, in *Shemot* 20:7.)

According to the most traditional approach, then, the last statement of the first tablet is to honor one's parents. From here on, we encounter a very terse list of "don'ts." The clear-cut, unnuanced nature of the last five commandments is only one of the differences between the two halves of the Decalogue that should strike us. Among others is the well-known distinction made by many

20 *Mechilta, Shemot* 20:13; *Shemot Rabba* 47:6.

commentators[21] that the first set has to do with commandments between man and God and the second set focuses on those between man and man.[22]

The opinion that the tablets were divided into two sections of five each beautifully embodies the conceptual split just mentioned, but it is quite visually dissonant. The obvious lack of symmetry in terms of the number of words on each tablet – with the first being far more wordy than the second – requires explanation. We know that symmetry is part of the natural world and can often be found in the Tanach as well.[23] Moreover, the Masoretic division mentioned above parenthetically does break down the two sections in this manner, dividing the fourteen verses of the Decalogue quite neatly both mathematically and visually, with seven in the first section and seven in the second. Hence, there has to be a very good reason – which we believe to be the case here – to push such an important stylistic tool aside.

Five Plus Five Equal One

Perhaps even more significant than the differences between the two sections of the Ten Statements is what they have in common. First and foremost is the fact that each set of commandments, i.e., those between man and God and those that focus on interpersonal relationships, is given its own tablet. By doing so, the Torah is going out of its way to give equal weight to these two sections. Moreover, as R. Yoel bin Nun points out, each set contains exactly six negative commandments, reinforcing our sense that the Torah is trying to create some sort of organizational symmetry out of these two otherwise disparate units.

Consequently, half of the document we are examining – conceptually

21 See, for example, Ramban, *Bemidbar* 20:12.

22 Honoring parents is associated with the former, even though there is room to understand this commandment as part of the latter. Nevertheless, stylistically it certainly belongs to the first half, and hence almost all commentators feel motivated to interpret it in that light regardless. Ramban points out that it is *also* the first of the commandments between man and man, even though it is ultimately related to the honor of God and, therefore, rightfully finds its place on the first tablet.

23 We only need to examine the design of the Tabernacle and priestly garments to see the balance that exists in most of their components.

speaking – is given over to how God expects man to treat his fellow man. Even if this represents the second set of five commandments, we see no gradation between the two – of a larger and a smaller tablet, for instance, or anything of that type. Rather, the Torah just calls them the – seemingly parallel – "Two Tablets of the Covenant."[24]

This equality is particularly striking in light of the Decalogue's being given as an expression of Divine power mentioned earlier. As we suggested, the giving of the Ten Statements was a type of swearing-of-loyalty ceremony, parallel to that undergone by ancient vassals toward their suzerains. In that situation the clear focus was on loyalty to the suzerain. Here, however, the Ten Statements want to provide symmetry between loyalties to the ultimate Suzerain on the one hand and basic morality toward one's fellow man on the other. This is as significant as it is unusual.

It is not only in relation to ancient political documents that this balance is striking. After all, a human king making a covenant with his subjects serves as but a pale metaphor for the relationship between God and human beings. One would think that God would demand much more attention to His own service than would a human king. Contemplating the true greatness of God leads one to imagine that there is actually only one truly meaningful relationship in our lives – the one with Him.[25] Hence, had we humans constructed the Ten Statements we might well have left the entire "second tablet" for a different occasion.

With the two tablets, God has made an almost startling statement about interpersonal morality. To be able to make more sense of it, it helps to remember that although there are two tablets, they are first and foremost one entity of legislation between man and God. This means that ultimately *all* Ten Statements are related to the service of God. Yet this only strengthens the question: In what way is interpersonal morality so central to the obedience to God?

In Jewish tradition, God is often compared to a human father. Continuing

24 See *Shemot Rabba* 41:6 and especially the commentary of Rabbi Shmuel Yaffe Ashkenazi, *Yefat Toar*.
25 See Francis Nataf, *Redeeming Relevance in the Book of Genesis* (Jerusalem: Urim Publications, 2006), Chapter Four.

the metaphor, stealing from another human being would be an affront to his or her "Father in heaven" in the same way as stealing from a child is really stealing from that child's father. The metaphor is particularly apt here, for not only is a child loved and cherished by his parents, he is legally within his parents' financial domain. He is also created by them in their own image. Indeed, an attack on one's child is often experienced by the parent more harshly than an attack on the parent himself.

Accordingly, God resembles a father at least as much as He resembles a king. For what flesh and blood sovereign would really care as much about how his subjects treat each other as he does about how they treat him? But a *father* does care as much about how his son is treated as he cares about how he himself is treated.

It is not only that God differentiates Himself from human leaders, as much as it is that He clearly establishes the general contours of what He expects from His subjects. The notion of God's preeminent interest in how people treat each other, implanted as it is in the Ten Statements, leads the rabbis to make other, somewhat shocking statements with regard to the centrality of interpersonal commandments, even in comparison with commandments toward God. For example, when Avraham is speaking with God, the rabbis understand that he appropriately interrupted his interview in order to tend to his ostensibly human guests.[26] They likewise read a hint in the words of the prophet Yirmiyahu that suggests God allows His own honor to take second place to the carrying out of His commandments.[27]

In the midst of the austere and fearful drama that was *Ma'amad Har Sinai*, God makes sure to introduce a new way of looking at obedience to the ultimate King and ruler. Obedience means not only how one should treat Him, but equally, how one should treat His children.

* * *

We have seen that the Ten Statements are actually much more complex than often thought and include some important aspects we might not have

---

26 *Shevuot* 35b.
27 *Eichah Rabba*, Introduction:2 on *Yirmiyahu* 16:11.

considered before. Among them is that more important than the text of the Ten Commandments is its context, which is a ceremony designed to bring appreciation for the absolute nature of the loyalty that Jews are expected to show to God. Once that is understood, the choice of commandments contained follows more readily, as we described.

But even more significant is our understanding of why they are divided into two equal tablets, the first containing laws of obedience to God and the second containing interpersonal laws. Given its lack of visual symmetry, we discovered that a major statement is being made – that God cares as much about how we treat each other as how we treat Him. While the central place of interpersonal ethics in Judaism is already well known, that it is actually rooted in *Maʾamad Har Sinai* gives it an even more fundamental place still.

This is not without practical ramifications. As religious people, it is imperative that we remember the apparently surprising orientation that God Himself provides us in the Ten Statements. On the one hand, He expects our absolute fealty and dedication. On the other hand, precisely because of that fealty He expects us to treat others as His own children. Failing to do so is not only an ethical failing; it is an act of total insubordination toward the same God Who demands and expects our absolute allegiance.

CHAPTER 4

The *Shema* and all that Jazz

MANY OF US are not immediately struck by the greatness of the Mona Lisa upon first seeing it. In fact, when encountering any classic work for the first time we often fail to see what the fuss is all about.

Sometimes greatness is in the details, as with the six verses that form the first paragraph of what we refer to as the *Shema* (*Devarim* 6:4–9). The casual reader may not immediately pick up on why this little section has taken such pride of place in the Jewish liturgy. For one, the Torah doesn't present it with the same fanfare given the Ten Commandments, the second version of which precedes this passage by about ten verses. Nor is its meaning so unequivocal that the reader would necessarily even understand much of it – at least not without some difficulty.

Yet most of us take it for granted that this passage is quite important. Even beyond the obligation to read it at least twice a day (which can reasonably be understood from the text itself[1]), it plays a rather impressive role in the life of a Jew. For one, that these six verses are the words which a Jew should recite on his deathbed certainly gives it a stature incomparable to any other passage in the Torah. But it is not only saved for the grand finale; its recitation upon going to sleep both foreshadows and hints to its being a Jew's last word. Likewise, its central positioning in the prayer service – ensconced between several blessings assigned to it – shows it to be the main word as well.

Given the disparity between the *Shema*'s central place in Jewish tradition

---

1   *Devarim* 6:7.

and its nondescript presentation in the Torah, we need to better understand the roots of its renown. In the process, we will be able to get better insight into a large part of Moshe's parting speeches, of which the *Shema* is an integral part.

The Jazz of the *Shema* Unit

A close reading of the first paragraph of the *Shema* and an examination of its context reveal a great deal. With regard to its placement within the book of *Devarim*, it precedes the second paragraph of the *Shema* by five chapters (11:13–20). The two passages cover much the same ground, something we will discuss in greater detail later in the chapter.

The first two paragraphs of the *Shema* are atypical of repetitive biblical passages. Generally, repetitive passages are either right next to each other or separated by many chapters or even whole books. They usually consist of almost the exact same content. What's more, because the second passage is repeated in a new context, it is stated for reasons different from those of the first. Here, however, we have something quite different.

For one, the passages are neither immediately adjacent to each other nor far removed from one another. Moreover, the passages, while quite similar in content and meaning, are uniquely stylized: certain phrases in the first passage are omitted in the second, new passages are inserted into the second that did not appear in the first, and grammatical schemes differ.

In addition to the particulars of their specific content, these sections also bookend what others have already identified as the fundamental "mitzva" section of Moshe's discourse (*Devarim* 6:4–11:25).[2] The primary theme of "the mitzva" is basic allegiance, and it is quite clear that we are dealing with a distinct thematic section which opens with the first paragraph of the *Shema* and concludes with the second, and is all about the need to be loyal to God.

---

2   See *Recalling the Covenant*, pp. 897– 903. See also R. David Zvi Hoffman's introduction to his commentary to *Devarim*, where he says that this section deals with "general commandments."

When these elements combine with the fact that the verses between these two passages have much the same substance and style as their "bookends," we see something quite singular being created. At the very least, the Torah has brought the different pieces together to create a larger thematic section of text. But I believe it is actually much more.

An objection could be raised that this unit appears to be highly unwieldy and has parts that don't fit very well with the general theme. Yet not all patterns and themes work in the same way. In fact, sometimes a certain amount of disorder is itself a part of the art. For those familiar with jazz music, this may ring a bell.

The entire passage (i.e., *Devarim* 6:7–11:20) actually has some very striking affinities with jazz. For one, a jazz composition begins and returns to a common, unifying theme. Moreover, the final rendition of the theme at the conclusion of the piece is usually presented in a different, somewhat more robust form. The latter is exactly what we find in the second paragraph of the *Shema*. Even more helpful is what we find in the middle section, between the bookends. As in jazz, the binding thread is not always easy to follow and sometimes even leads to a complete tangent. Nevertheless, we get constant reminders of it, with variations of the theme's components finding their way into key parts of the composition, most commonly at points of transition.

Along these lines, the phrase, "the Lord, your God," which we find in the second verse of the *Shema*, is found clustered throughout the entire section. Most notably, it appears five times in five different verses early on and seven times in the course of seven other verses a bit later.[3] Immediately after the first occurrence of "The Lord, your God" comes *bechol levavecha u'vechol nafshecha* (with all of your heart and with all of your soul). This too is pointedly repeated[4] in the middle section, as is the very famous beginning of the section, *Shema Yisrael* (Listen, Israel).[5] Both these last two phrases reappear only once,

---

3   Ibid., 6:12–16, 7:19–25. This phrase is rarely used in the other four books of the Torah, but frequently used in other parts of *Devarim*. Still, it appears with slightly greater frequency here than in the rest of the book.

4   Ibid., 10:12. The word *levavecha* by itself is sprinkled several times throughout this section as well.

5   Ibid., 8:1.

but given their very uncommon word combinations, it is hard to see their repetition as mere coincidence.[6]

As mentioned, a jazz piece reverts to its main theme at the very end. It does so because the melody that begins and ends the song informs the essence of the piece. The same can be said of our text as well: The central purpose of the repetition at the end, as well as of its various strands that emerge in the middle, is to demarcate the larger unit's major theme.[7]

Admittedly, there are parts of the "mitzva" section where the main pattern is less clear; the discussion of the golden calf incident immediately comes to mind. But I would suggest that the atypical parts can be likened to jazz riffs. And so, when looking at the entire piece, a pattern comes through clearly – one made up of various components that create a very sophisticated thematic unit.

Singular and Plural

Now that we better understand the unity of the section we are studying, it is time to find its message. Instead of looking to rhythmic patterns, however, here we will examine grammatical ones. The first of this three-part unit uses verbs exclusively in the singular form, thereby addressing the individual Israelite. Significantly, however, these singular verbs gradually give way to an increasing use of the plural – meaning to all the Jews as a nation – which comes to a head with the ending paragraph being almost completely in the plural.

The middle section goes back and forth – sometimes including more plural verbs, sometimes less – and therefore it would be difficult for us to make much of the gradual shift from singular to plural were it to be our only piece of evidence.[8] There are, however, several other items that combine to address

6   The expression appears five times altogether, all of them in the book of *Devarim*.
7   While many of these patterns exist to one extent or another throughout Moshe's speeches in *Devarim*, they seem to come together most powerfully in this section. One could say that this section forms a more concentrated microcosm of what Moshe is trying to get across throughout his speeches as a whole.
8   See Rabbi S.R. Hirsch, *Devarim* 11:10, who points out that this is a feature seen

the relationship between the individual and the collective. To begin with, the most widely repeated phrase, "the Lord, your God," is used revealingly. In general, the phrase is meant to emphasize the relationship we have with God, but to the extent that the word "you" is conspicuously found here much more often in the singular than in the plural, God is creating expectations of what He wants specifically from each individual. Hence the religious responsibility of the Jew does not only begin on the individual level, but on a very basic level it remains there as well.

And just as the singular (representing the individual) continues to have a role even as we progress into the plural (representing the community), the same is true in reverse. From the very beginning, we are given an indication that the message of allegiance is not only directed to the individual. In fact, this happens at the very beginning of the first "bookend" with the introductory expression, *Shema Yisrael*, for here we also go from the individual verb *Shema* to the collective noun *Yisrael*. This phrase sets the tone for the entire section; its words speak of a communal listening predicated on its internalization by each individual member (the word *shema* connotes not just listening but a comprehension and acceptance of that which is heard). For that internalization to happen, each individual must feel that the message is directed specifically to him or her, and that it is not just a general mandate for the Jewish people as a whole.[9]

Every individual must see himself as the one being addressed in the *Shema*, yet if he sees it only that way he will be missing the point: in order to succeed we need to pay attention to both the group and to its component parts. In spite of the centrality of all Jews feeling personally addressed, each one must concurrently internalize that the full scope of their loyalty to God is expressed communally.

This idea comes out even more strongly in a well-known verse that has

---

throughout Moshe's orations in the book of *Devarim*. See also Aharon Mirsky's commentary to the book of *Devarim* in *Da'at Mikra* (Jerusalem: Mossad HaRav Kook, 2001), pp. 36–37, and previous footnote.

9   In *Devarim* 29:18–19, Moshe specifically addresses the likelihood that some will excuse themselves from following the commandments of the Torah, based on the sense that what really matters to God is the group as a whole, and not the individual.

posed difficulties for many a reader.[10] The verse in question is borrowed by the Passover Haggadah and there attributed to the "wise son": "What are the statutes and laws and judgments that the Lord, *our* God, commanded *you* [plural]?" Even though the son is speaking as a member of the community and the father is addressed as a representative of the community, the Torah still presents a singular son speaking to a singular father.

The essence of this passage serves as an almost perfect example of the interplay between the individual and the group. For here we see the transmission of the Torah's laws on a national basis, by *individuals* who recognize the *national* scope of this process. The actual and literal transmissions occur only one family at a time; it is a specific, individual son who will ask his specific, individual father. Yet it is an event that must be replicated in many thousands of households for it to have the communal meaning it actually expresses.

In the unit we are analyzing, Moshe is subtly trying to expand the horizons of singularity in order to convince the Jews of the idea that the self is really the collective self at least as much as it is the singular one. Moshe will not deny that it is individuals who constitute groups, but the group made up of individuals needs to coalesce and become a community. In that scenario, individuals enhance the power of their commitments by fulfilling them together.

The Righteous Men of Sodom

The group cannot function without the many individuals who ultimately and individually make their own choices. By the same token, if these choices are made without concern for the group, they can carry only so much significance. This is best demonstrated in the book of *Bereshit*, in the argument between Avraham and God about Sodom. There it is manifest that the presence of

---

10 Ibid., 6:20. The problem is why we think of him as such a wise son if he excludes himself from the community that received the laws, especially since the "evil son" was seemingly just castigated for doing the exact same thing. In the context of the Torah's presentation, the answer is quite clear. The Torah is describing a father who witnessed the Exodus from Egypt, saying the miracles "happened in front of our eyes" (v. 22); and a son who did not witness it.

one or two righteous individuals is not enough to warrant Sodom's continued existence. Avraham is aware of that and asks nothing more of God once it comes down to there being less than ten righteous individuals in the city. The only point in question is how large a minority is needed to create a suitably representative subcommunity.[11] Once there is less than a quorum, the individual will, at best, be taken out of the city (as was Lot) and judged on his own merits.[12] In the worst case, he will be held accountable for continuing to live in the face of evil, which he was either not able or not willing to change.[13]

But even if such an individual is deemed guiltless, he still does not define the merits of his *community*. Rather, it is the group that defines the aggregate actions of the community and, subsequently, whether that community is helping or hindering mankind's moral growth and welfare.

Indeed, being part of a nation is what makes people proud to fight just wars or to develop exemplary health care systems. That pride is felt by the masses, even though most of the individuals did not take part in carrying out the task. Likewise, if a nation is plagued by rampant crime, vice and blatant inequalities, most citizens are embarrassed by the problems even if they themselves are among the guiltless. Both the pride and the shame arise from the understanding that they belong to a group that is making an impact beyond only those that comprise the group. Even more to the point is that this feeling arises from the knowledge that this achievement can only be attained on the communal level. Hence the greatest influence an average individual can make is usually when he acts as part of the larger community.

In light of this, the Jewish community's commitment can be more fully understood. We have mentioned before that God's selection of the Jews has a twofold purpose: to elevate the members of the Jewish nation and thereby produce moral and religious excellence, and to provide an example for the rest of mankind.[14]

---

11 See Rabbi S.R. Hirsch, *Bereshit* 18:28, concerning the implications of the numbers of righteous inhabitants in Sodom.

12 See Ramban, *Devarim* 11:13, and the next section of this chapter.

13 See *Sanhedrin* 112a, which not only blames a righteous person for continuing to live in such a situation but also penalizes him financially.

14 See *Redeeming Relevance in Exodus*, pp. 57–67.

A truly outstanding individual can be an inspiration for some individuals, but he cannot be a model for an entire nation to duplicate. When it comes to individuals, it is understood that there will always be some whose performance is off the charts. A nation cannot hold itself to such a standard, since it will be unattainable for the average citizen. A model nation, however, is something else.

E Pluribus Unum

Now that we have seen and explored the patterned use of singular and plural in our section, we can return to the most obvious difference between the two sections of the *Shema* that serve as bookends for the "mitzva paragraphs" of the book of *Devarim*. As many have noticed before,[15] the second bookend begins in the singular and ends mostly in the plural, an indication of a clear *progression* from the one to the other which is, in light of what we have observed, expected. This progression strongly reinforces the need to begin with the pole of individuality and only then to move forward toward the pole of community.

While this idea is always true, the Torah rarely feels the need to emphasize it. There must then be something about this particular unit, in which the first two parts of the *Shema* encompass the "mitzva paragraphs," which warrants the particular emphasis on the centrality of the many individuals required to constitute the group. With this in mind, we begin to understand why this section is so important. For this is where Moshe is telling the Jews God's bottom line. He describes what commitment will entail with regard to dealing with their children and with their neighbors. He also tells them of the protection and bounty they can expect from God in return. But the Torah doesn't stop with the positive. It also reminds the Jews that there is another side, explaining what they can expect if they don't maintain their part of the bargain. Most important here is the message that it is ultimately upon this commitment that the fate of the Jews *as a nation* will rest. In order to assure the nation's survival,

---

15   See, for example, *Sifrei*; Rashi; Ramban, *Devarim* 11:13.

and hopefully its success, Moshe now needs to ensure that the nation is in a communally directed and alert state of mind.

The commitment required from the *nation* can be boiled down to two verses in the middle of this section: "Now, Israel, what does the Lord, your God, demand from you except to fear the Lord, your God, to walk in His ways and to love Him, and to serve the Lord, your God, with all your heart and with all your soul, and to keep the *mitzvot* of the Lord and His *chukim*, which I command you this day for your good? (*Devarim* 10:12–13). These essentially speak of a proper attitude toward God and complete obedience to His will.

The diction in the Hebrew implies that this isn't really so much to ask, to which the rabbis respond, "That's easy for him (Moshe) to say!"[16] The end of verse 13 already tells us why the commitment is not as hard as it sounds: obedience is in the Jews' clear and obvious self-interest. Since God's law is meant to be a guide to a better, more correct and more rewarding life, there is no rational reason not to follow it.

Complete and total obedience can never be a simple matter, but whether simple or not, it is what God unequivocally requires of His people. This is the message that led the rabbis to mandate a Jew's willingness to die for the greater good – which specifically means to do God's will – while reciting the *Shema*.[17] For it is precisely in life-or-death situations more than at any other time that the nation needs its individuals to stand up and be counted.

This message, which Jewish martyrs have embodied in actual practice throughout history, is actually in the text itself, in the second verse of the first passage. But the centrality of this section as a whole cued the rabbis to establish its use whenever a Jew is required to declare his loyalty. Indeed, it was to become the Jews' loyalty oath.

An oath of loyalty actually provides us with a very useful metaphor here. Such declarations are what bind individuals to groups. Even while the *Shema* is primarily directed toward God, it is no coincidence that the *Shema* is

---

16 *Berachot* 33b.

17 See *Bach* on *Tur, Orach Chaim* 61, which cites *Vayikra Rabba* 27:6. Though unclear whether this is the intention of the Midrash, or even necessarily of *Tur*, it has become generally accepted. See *Aruch HaShulchan* 61:1; *Mishna Berura* 3; *Kaf HaChaim* 6, both on *Shulchan Aruch, Orach Chaim* 61:1.

frequently recited together with a group. As we shall see, it is the type of activity that generally only makes sense when performed by the many. For what does it matter if only one or two soldiers swear fealty to the king or the state?

The *Shema* in Plural

The general patterns we have noticed also address some of the major differences that exist between the first paragraph of *Shema* and its adaptation in the second. Among the most important is the discussion of reward, which is completely absent from the former and emphasized in the latter. In this context, let us examine a curious statement of Rashi's and follow it up with an elaboration from Ramban and others.

Obviously aware that the two paragraphs cover much the same ground, Rashi immediately cites a Midrash which tells us that one is a warning to the individual and the other is a warning to the group.[18] One might think Rashi is just restating the obvious difference we have also traced, yet, as many supercommentaries point out,[19] all commandments are ultimately the responsibility of the individual, and to the extent that communal responsibility is involved in making sure that others also follow the commandments, it ostensibly applies to all commandments equally and not merely the ones laid out in these two paragraphs.

Ramban addresses this problem by pointing out that none of the consequences here, such as abundant rainfall, can be called an open miracle (*nes nigleh*); the miraculous nature of any consequence mentioned in the *Shema* becomes evident only when the entire nation is reaping it. In other words, the reward itself is not immediately apparent and could be attributed to chance. Ramban calls this type of phenomenon a hidden miracle (*nes nistar*).

According to Ramban, the physical rewards described in the second paragraph of the *Shema* can follow only in the wake of the acts of many individuals. God has an interest in showing His approval of the Jewish people when

---

18 Rashi, based on *Sifrei, Devarim* 11:13.
19 See, for example, *Siftei Chachamim*; Maharal (*Gur Aryeh*) ad loc.

they follow His laws by granting them the type of success that other nations will want. Miracles are to be noticed and the actions leading to them are to be emulated. This scenario provides an ideal mechanism: it is not so obvious as to remove free will but noticeable enough to bring about serious reflection. In any event, the mechanism plays itself out on the group level. Hence, there is ample reason for Divine recompense to be associated only with the paragraph that speaks about the group and not with the one that speaks to the individual.

Another noteworthy difference between the two paragraphs in question is the exclusion of *me'odecha* ("your possessions")[20] from the set of commitments expected from the group.[21] People usually pay less attention to the expenditures of the state than to the effort and human resources claimed by national causes. On the contrary, it is not uncommon for citizens to be unconcerned about lavish expenses when it is on the state's tab. Hence, although it makes sense for the individual to be commanded to spend his very last earnings for the sake of God and the mitzvot if need be, asking the same of the community does not add much to the demand for its will and manpower already stated in the second paragraph of the *Shema*.

The two differences we have just examined further establish the pattern of movement from a group of righteous individuals to a righteous nation. Together with everything we have seen so far, it becomes even more evident that going from the individual to the group is a fundamental part of the Jewish mission. It is now only left for us to briefly review this entire three-part unit's central place in the Jewish liturgy and tradition.

The Pledge of Allegiance to the Mission

The Jews' obligation of loyalty to God demanded in this section of *Devarim* is far from a private affair. It is not merely that this obligation can never really

---

20 The exact meaning of this word is unclear, and we have followed the popular rabbinic understanding. See *Berachot* 54a.

21 See Rabbi S.R. Hirsch, ibid., and *Recalling the Covenant*, p. 904, both of whom are of the opinion that it is replaced by the phrase of *ule'ovdo* (and to serve Him), which they feel is essentially the same thing.

get off the ground if it remains on the individual level. The more crucial problem is that if loyalty to God would remain in the realm of the individual, the ensuing heterogeneity would disable the central mission for which the Jews were chosen, which is to provide an example to the rest of the world. This is the reason Jews must recite the three paragraphs of the *Shema* in this specific order – to show their understanding of the pressing need for them to be a member of the group.

The first two paragraphs of the *Shema* summarize the larger unit, i.e., these paragraphs plus the "mitzva" section of *Devarim* they encompass. The entire passage is too hard to remember and too unwieldy to focus on with proper intention two or more times a day. Nevertheless, by invoking the introduction and conclusion, which together define the main theme, the Jew is making the full declaration of all that is included in the greater passage.

With these two summary paragraphs, the Jew pronounces his loyalty to God. In doing so, he is declaring loyalty to his national mission as well. He is announcing and internalizing that his commitment to God is not just a rational move of self-interest or a glib declaration of knowledge. It is part of something much larger. It is speaking to his identity as part of a nation with a mission no less than the redemption of all mankind. With this in mind, the Jew must stand up and be counted as part of God's nation, or not be counted at all.

CHAPTER 5

Kings and the Problem of Professionalization

AMONG THE LAWS found in the book of *Devarim* for the first time are those concerning the sociopolitical organization of the new Jewish state. They include the rights and duties of kings, proper conduct of war and the appointment of law enforcers. The reason for the appearance of these laws specifically now is obvious; they are among the laws that would become relevant only when the Jews entered the land, and thus did not need to be taught until right before their entry. As mentioned earlier, many commentators have found this to be the organizing principle with regard to which laws are chosen to be included in the final book of the Torah.[1]

Yet there is another possible reason for the late appearance of the laws of statecraft. If economics is often described as the "dismal science," politics may, in fact, be an even more dismal discipline still. Although this central area of life must be addressed in the Torah, it is likely done reluctantly. Whatever system and laws are set up in the sociopolitical realm will inevitably be misused – that being the nature of the beast.

There are many ways in which this reluctance to set up a sociopolitical system is felt. In our first volume, we discussed the intrinsic problem of human political power and why true Jewish leaders come to leadership with great ambivalence. We wrote that these reticent leaders understand that power over

---

1   See Chapter 2, page 37.

others is suited, ultimately, only for God. Only He can truly know what is good for others and how to effect that good.[2] Still, He created man in such a way that he would need to build societies with human leaders. And as many political philosophers have pointed out, the great evil that comes out of political power is nevertheless outweighed by the good that results from it.

The Torah's ultimate ideal is a state in which people are enlightened enough not to need the leadership of others.[3] But ideals should not be confused with the need for guidelines for the practical, "real" world until and unless the ideals can be realized. Therefore, it was essential for the Torah to give us some guidance on how to create the best parameters for the administration of a state.

What's Wrong with a King?

Many commentators have already noted the strange language that introduces the commandment to appoint a king. It is first couched against the usually questionable backdrop of the Jews wanting to be like all the nations around them.[4] Moreover, the Torah mandates the appointment of a king only if the Jews actually request it.[5] From at least the time of the Talmud, many careful readers of the Torah have seen this, among other things, as a sign of the Torah's ambivalence – or worse – toward a Jewish king.[6]

The Torah's hesitation concerning a Jewish king anticipates an inherent problem with having one, and foresees that this problem can be only mitigated but not removed. Consequently, it establishes limits on what often leads to abuse; first and foremost, money and women. The Torah also proscribes a third item, the accumulation of too many horses, ostensibly aimed at limiting

2 *Redeeming Relevance in Genesis*, pp. 114–119.
3 See *Redeeming Relevance in Numbers*, pp. 58–59.
4 *Devarim* 17:14.
5 See *Ha'amek Davar*, ibid.
6 See *Sanhedrin* 20b, which engenders a debate among commentators on the books of *Devarim* and *II Shmuel*. See also Eric Nelson, *The Hebrew Republic* (Cambridge, MA: Harvard University Press, 2010), which traces the influence of this tradition on proto-Enlightenment Christian thinkers who begin their critique of contemporary monarchy based upon it.

contact with the primary source of this commodity, Israel's cradle and nemesis, Egypt.[7] Moreover, since horses were the ancient equivalent of heavy weaponry, this could well have had the ancillary benefit of controlling the potential hubris that could occur when leaders have more weaponry than they need.

In addition to what a king should not do (or possess) comes an extra requirement of what he needs *to* do. He must always keep God's demands in mind, and in order to facilitate this he is required to carry a Torah scroll wherever he goes. We will return to these safeguards, both the do's and the don'ts, but we must first understand why the Torah was so concerned in the first place.

The place to begin is with the crowning of the first Israelite king. Significantly, it is several centuries after receiving the Torah until the Jewish polity actually appoints a monarch.[8] This in and of itself seems to be an indication of the Jewish tradition's ambivalence toward monarchy. But if reticence is only implicit up to that point, the establishment of a united monarchy brings outright opposition from the Torah's then main exponent, the prophet Shmuel.

In fact, the monarchy's initial implementation in the book of *Shmuel* is one of the Bible's most dramatic moments. When the Jewish people come to ask Shmuel for a king, his reaction is nothing short of hysterical: He tells them of the near-slavery that a king will impose upon them and how their request is, in any case, a great sin.[9] Were his words not so vivid we could say that the special effects of conjuring up a storm in the midst of the dry season speak even louder.[10] In any event, the esteemed prophet's reaction makes it hard to see the establishment of monarchy as a welcome event, so much so that those rabbis and commentators who defend monarchy are hard-pressed to find an explanation for Shmuel's vehement opposition.

Essentially, their answer is that Shmuel's concerns were localized to the specifics involved. They claim that the motivations of the group that came to

---

7 See *Redeeming Relevance in Exodus*, Chapter One.
8 See *Ha'amek Davar, Devarim* 17:14. Netziv is one of the few classical commentators who addresses this issue head on.
9 *I Shmuel* 8.
10 Ibid., Chapter 12.

Shmuel were the real problem, not the establishment of a monarchy *per se*.[11] This theory is certainly possible, but it is not the most obvious reading of the story.

Based on Shmuel's own words, the brunt of the debate about the desirability of a monarch is actually about whether such an office shows a lack of trust in God. After all, the main role of a king is to protect his nation and advance its economic interests. Did God not already do that for the Jews? Indeed, in "consoling" Shmuel, God reinforces this idea by telling him that "it is not you they are rejecting but rather Me."[12] But this is not the final word.

The problem with a Jewish monarchy according to some commentators goes beyond a simple reading of Shmuel's opposition. For Abarbanel, for instance, the form of government was the true problem. Having been an insider in the Spanish monarchy and also having gone through Spain's expulsion of the Jews, Abarbanel's generalized opposition to monarchy is easy to imagine. And not only did he see the weaknesses and failings of several monarchies, he also saw what appeared to be a much better alternative when he immigrated to republican Venice at the height of its glory.

In light of his experiences, Abarbanel understood the Torah to be warning the Jews not to fall into the common trap of thinking that a monarch will provide more effective leadership than a system wherein leadership is shared and can be more easily monitored and checked.[13] But while Abarbanel correctly looks at the ultimate failure of Biblical Jewish monarchy, his condemnation is somewhat problematic. Even if he is correct in his reading of the historical Jewish monarchy, he fails to explain why the Torah does not at least *suggest* what he views to be a better type of government.

11 *Sanhedrin* 20b. See Michael Walzer, *In God's Shadow* (New Haven: Yale University Press, 2012), Chapter 4, which does a good job of tracing the rival Jewish traditions about the monarchy.

12 *I Shmuel* 8:7. Of course, this type of reasoning can be taken *ad absurdum*. Should the Jews not plow and sow but rather simply place their faith in God? Although such a line of thinking is not completely foreign to Jewish tradition, it is fairly marginal; see *Berachot* 35b. See also Rambam's *Commentary to the Mishna, Pesachim* 4:10, which uses the absurdity of such an idea as a rhetorical flourish.

13 Abarbanel, *I Shmuel* 8:6.

I believe the Bible had something else in mind. Although we will also examine the Biblical record, we must look broader and deeper than the textual analysis suggested by Abarbanel's conclusion. Ironically, a broader perspective will show that the Bible's most critical objection to monarchy is much simpler than Abarbanel's theory.

But it is not only with Abarbanel that I take issue on this topic. The lack of trust in God which many other commentators have concluded to be the main problem is not without its own difficulties either. Besides looking for lessons relevant to our times, one of the main reasons I am seeking a novel explanation is that a straightforward reading of Shmuel's critique of not relying upon God's direct rule makes it doomed from the start. The direct rule of God simply appears to be more than what the Israelites can handle. If so, is there not a more relevant and effective critique that can apply when all states, Jewish or gentile, will necessarily be administered by powerful human leaders? Let us look at the Biblical record more carefully.

Proto-Division of Religion and State

It is obvious that the first king, Shaul, presented a new model for Jewish governance. Less obvious are the many ramifications of the model as viewed through the prophetic lens of the Bible. We are immediately aware that much more than the judges before him, King Shaul is a successful military and political leader. And yet it doesn't take much analysis to discover that he is also a terribly weak character. We see this in his remarkable unawareness of his own mistakes which, in turn, set the stage for frequent Divine rebuke.

But here the Bible employs a change in the order of things. As opposed to earlier leaders, each time Shaul does something wrong it is neither God nor one of His angels that comes to rebuke him. Rather, the Divine voice needs to be mediated. In this case, it is mediated by the prophet Shmuel, who eventually informs Shaul of God's decision to replace him. This reaches tragic proportions after Shmuel dies. Finding no other avenue to discover what God wants from him, Shaul feels he has no choice but to conjure Shmuel back from the dead.[14] In fact, this strange need for mediation with God seems to be part and parcel of the new leadership model Shaul represents, which is epitomized by Michael Walzer's poignant observation that "henceforth, God's interests are represented by the prophet."[15]

Even though things would be less dramatic in the subsequent reign of David, the die had already been cast – the externalization of religious criticism that was so clear with Shaul would typify all subsequent kings of Israel and Yehudah. From the best to the worst, Jewish kings would lack the inner voice of God – a voice that was integral to Jewish leadership up until that point. This comes through quite clearly in the lives of several of the earlier leaders, collectively known as the judges.

Israel's model judge, Gidon, was in frequent conversation with God. Likewise Devorah, another famous judge and prophetess.[16] This was also clearly the case with the first and last of the judges, Yehoshua and Shmuel (who is considered the last of the judges, even though he is significantly more well known for his role as a prophet), respectively. We don't know a great deal about many of the minor judges who led the Jewish people between Yehoshua and Shmuel, yet neither do we read about any of them being rebuked by prophets, as would be the case later with the kings.

The judges generally did not receive extended prophecy, but this had little to do with their ability to connect with the Divine. It is more likely a consequence of the relative simplicity of those times. The period of the judges was one of a great repetitive cycle: the Jews failed to live up to their potential, were reminded of their failures by being attacked and consequently subjugated by their enemies, and eventually respond with repentance, which brings about salvation led by a new judge.

Almost never was the judge himself the source of the evil. The spiritual level of the judges generally just reflected that of their followers and, if anything, was a cut above the level of their flock. Thus, we never see among the

14 *I Shmuel* 28:3–25.
15 Walzer, *In God's Shadow*, p. 67.
16 *Shoftim* 4:4.

judges the likes of a Yerav'am, who stops the people from going to the Temple in Jerusalem. Neither do we see a Menashe, who aggressively pushes the people toward idol worship. The Jews and their judges were already intuitively aware of their mistakes, and when things got really bad they turned to God, promising to do better in the future. The main role of the leadership at this time was to help the people with repentance and with their subsequent military deliverance. And this is exactly what the judges did, some better, some worse.

Not so with the kings. Not only did they not help the Jews avoid sin, they were often its cause. Why? We noted that a king's connection to God was externalized and that he would need to depend on a prophet for feedback. We will now seek to understand what made these new Jewish leaders less connected to God than their predecessors and consequently so much more susceptible to moral corruption.

Who was the judge? As opposed to the king, he was essentially apolitical. He neither sought leadership nor spent significant effort on its administration. He came to fulfill a temporary leadership task and, when it was finished, returned to private life. Even judges such as Yehoshua and Shmuel, who were heavily involved in leadership throughout their lives, did not set up much of an administration and did not seek to establish a coherent state apparatus. Hence, since less was expected from the judge politically, more could be expected spiritually, if for no other reason than he could afford the time and effort required to be a complete and well-integrated religious personality.

The king, however, was a true career man – someone we could describe as a political specialist. Sometimes, as in the case of David and Chizkiyahu, he was also a pious Jew. Other times, as in the case of Menashe, he was a rogue. But in either case he was too preoccupied with everything that goes into running a state to lead a properly focused religious life, not to mention to provide true religious leadership. In the best scenario he would need spiritual oversight. In the worst he would need to be stopped.

As it turns out, the religious oversight of kings came in the new form of the subversive prophet. Being independent of the leadership, the prophet was free to critique it – and, when necessary, even to undermine it. This was a novel development. So long as the leader had also been a prophet, as was the case with the patriarchs, Moshe and the judges, destabilizing Jewish regimes was not at all within the parameters of prophecy. Yet from Shmuel on, this would become a major part of the social and political landscape.

The clear distinction between the kings and the judges on the one hand, and the consistent pattern in the relationship between kings and prophets on the other, shows that it is the very institution of the Jewish monarchy that brought about the need for such an independent religious voice. The establishment of a professional head of state is the reason for the appearance of the subversive prophet. The institution of this type of prophet essentially arose as a system of checks and balances for what could be described as the now secularly focused leaders of the Jewish state.

The absence of prophecy in Jewish kings was not a personal shortcoming. Even the greatest of the kings were largely excluded from receiving prophecy. It is well known that when David marries Batsheva under questionable circumstances, God rebukes him through the prophet Natan rather than appearing to David directly.[17] Less well known is when David's other prophet, Gad, comes later on to remind him of his spiritual and moral obligations. While that story, which concerns David's census, is already recorded in the book of *II Shmuel*,[18] its later rendition in *II Divrei HaYamim* is even more revealing. There David speaks to God, but God only responds through the prophet.[19] Apparently, direct access to God is something even a king of David's caliber is unable, or perhaps not allowed, to have.

In this context, it should be pointed out that David's *Tehillim*, as well as his calls to God in other books of the Bible, are not prophetic. They might display a highly developed sense of religiosity, but that is not the same as being in direct communication with God.

David's son Shlomo may have been the one exception to this rule.[20] During

17 *II Shmuel* 12:1–14.

18 Ibid., 24:1–13.

19 *II Divrei HaYamim* 21:8–18.

20 Shaul also gets a modicum of prophecy at the beginning of his career, but it is couched in curious terms of surprise on his part, as if to say it's a freak spiritual accident. Another king who is described as receiving prophecy is Yehu (*II Melachim* 10:30), but Jewish tradition understands that this was not a case of direct prophecy but only one conveyed to him by the prophet Yonah (*Seder Olam* 19).

at least two points in his career he is addressed directly by God.[21] Whether that actually gives him the status of a prophet is less clear. (And, as with his father, authorship of great religious literature has no bearing on this.) Even if we accord Shlomo the standing of a prophet, he still requires spiritual oversight and rebuke from an external source. Though not explicit in the Biblical text, Jewish tradition declares that it is only through the prophet Achiyah that God announces His displeasure to Shlomo and declares that most of the kingdom will be taken away from his heirs.[22] But even if we consider Shlomo a true exception, the general pattern remains the same: the subversive prophet needs to oversee and critique the religious behavior of the civil leader.

The Costs of Professional Leadership

The establishment of a Jewish monarchy came to answer a historical need. We have demonstrated that the judges were less spiritually vulnerable, but there is no escaping the fact that they were also politically less effective. With the exception of Yehoshua, the entire period from Moshe to Shaul is found to have had a largely ineffective, though often more religiously sensitive political leadership. With the advent of the kings, this model was flipped on its head. The king, who needed to concentrate on affairs of state, was less connected to moral imperatives and more insulated from Divine rebuke. In time, this trend only reinforced itself. To the extent that the kings became used to their secular role and depended on the prophets to fill in the spiritual gaps, the secularity of the kings became even more pronounced.

This is not to say that the kings were given a break and that less was expected

---

21 See *I Melachim* 11:9, which states that God appeared to him twice. This presumably refers to ibid., 3:5–14, 9:2–9.

22 Ibid., 11:11–13. Although the simple reading of the text could easily be understood here as another example of direct prophecy to Shlomo, various traditional commentators explain that a careful reading indicates otherwise (see, for example, Kli Yakar; Radak; Abarbanel). Even if we were to differ with this explanation and say that this is an exception wherein God speaks His rebuke directly to a king, its exceptionality is reinforced by the surprise of these commentators, who apparently feel forced to understand it as following the general rule.

of them than of other prominent Jews. They were expected to toe the line like any other Jew and, because of their place in the limelight, perhaps even more. They were also expected to use their powers as king to enforce Jewish law and promote its spirit. But all of this was to be done only from the position of a religious layman. Religious leadership was neither required nor expected.

The Jewish king's exemption from spiritual leadership, however, should be understood as no more than a necessary evil. It is only because a man cannot focus on both the state and the spirit that he was excused from being a religious leader as well. At the same time, falling short of the, albeit impossible, ideal comes at a tremendous cost to the king and to his nation: it is almost impossible for a person to excel at something that is not his main and daily focus. In other words, we become what we do. If we lead troops into battle in order to kill other people – even when necessary and justified – it affects who we become. And this is the very reason why the most outstandingly religious king, David, was not allowed to build the Temple. He had become a warrior king. As such, he was a true hero to his people, but a different type of hero than what was required to build the Temple.[23]

While not every judge was a great role model, there is no question that as a group the judges remained much more loyal to the Torah and its tenets than the kings. And here we have the main reason for Biblical legislation that anticipates the difficulty a king will have in maintaining a proper sense of morality. No doubt the temptations that come from power are a major part of the Torah's concern as well, but this is far from being its only concern. The king's overwhelming preoccupation with statecraft and his corresponding inability to attend to the spiritual leadership are, at the very least, as responsible.

The main issue, then, is not with there being only one absolute leader, as Abarbanel suggests. Rather, there is an inherent problem with any professional leader or leaders who, in view of their assignment, must concentrate on statecraft. Although any occupation that becomes the entire, unhealthy focus of one's life can draw a person away from a Torah lifestyle, the statesman has two additional problems:

(1) Since putting the Torah's theory into practice on a societal level requires

---

23 *I Divrei Hayamim* 22:8.

great perseverance and patience, a statesman might be tempted to run things in a more "practical" way than that which the Torah dictates. The king is given broad extra-legal powers by Jewish law for precisely this reason,[24] but the Torah still limits what the king is allowed to do, and this will inevitably get in the way of a leader who just wants to get the job done.

A good king will by necessity be a workaholic. For even with the best of advisors, a state of just about any size represents a large and multi-faceted enterprise. To oversee it properly requires concerned interest and involvement in many different time-consuming matters.

(2) Being at the helm makes the king an automatic role model. His subjects will naturally look up to him and many will want to emulate him – especially if he is successful. This is particularly dangerous, as a king's success can sometimes paradoxically be the result of his violating the Torah, as when Shlomo was able to create many beneficial alliances specifically by marrying more wives than he was allowed.

A professional leader who is only indirectly connected to the moral impulse can easily turn into an Achav or a Menashe. Seeing this again and again with the kings of Israel and Yehudah, we get a clear indication that the type of separation of religion and state that was ushered in with the Jewish monarchy comes at a very high cost indeed.

The question of whether or not the Jewish nation can run without the type of professional leader that we have just described might be one of the reasons for the argument between those who feel appointing a king is commanded by God and those who feel it is not. Whatever the resolution to this dispute, the problematic need to separate between religion and state brought to the fore by a king must be noted, even if it cannot completely be stopped. By acknowledging the tradeoffs brought on by a professional leader, as the Bible does, we are in a better position to watch for them and do what we can to mitigate them. Moreover, even if the professionalization of the leadership

---

24 See *Mishneh Torah, Hilchot Melachim* 3:10– 5:3. See also *Derashot HaRan, derashah* 11, who makes this exact point. He says that the impractical nature of Jewish civil law essentially requires a secular authority with extra-legal powers.

may be necessary for certain times, the Bible makes it clear that we must never think of it as an ideal.

* * *

We have concentrated on the problems created for the professional states-man and have noted that most professionals will be confronted by similar, if somewhat less intense, challenges. Today, many jobs demand unprecedented amounts of time and involvement, and sometimes keeping the laws of the Torah can present an impediment to the best performance of our duties in the secular environment that characterizes most workplaces. This means that our daily work routines can easily prevent us from being fully integrated religious individuals. And the fact that we don't have prophets to represent the Divine critique of our actions makes the matter more difficult still.

So what is to be done? The most obvious, though not always practical an-swer is to limit ourselves to careers and job situations where we won't be con-fronted with these challenges. Yet, just as Jewish kings may have been needed in their time, Jewish society, especially in Israel, needs high-powered religious professionals today.

The first task is to be aware of the problem, even as one is not able to live the ideal. This means internalizing that contemporary society is not built in a spiritually ideal fashion. In an ideal society, there would be no professional head of state. And neither would there be professional lawyers or businessmen or architects. In such a society, people would study for and work in these jobs on an ad hoc basis. The judges who served only when they were needed would serve as the model for this. This may sound radical, unrealistic or both, yet it must be placed against the alternative to which we have become all too accustomed.

In an increasingly secularized and specialized society, practitioners are expected to get so involved in their professions that as a result they become amateurs at everything else, including their spiritual lives. In a society modeled on the judges, something would necessarily be lost, just as something was lost with regard to statecraft under the judges. But it still remains preferable. That being said, it also remains largely out of reach.

There are too many forces preventing most of us from living lives uncompromised by the professional requirements of our livelihoods. Unless and until that changes, we need to look at the extra laws of the king as a model for how to rein ourselves in and not allow our professional lives to lead us astray. In the face of the greatest temptations operating in the secular world, we, like the king, must put up extra barriers. And perhaps even more important, like him, we must take the Torah with us wherever we go. Whether it is making sure to read the *parashah* during one's commute, or breaking for half an hour in the middle of the day for a *daf yomi* podcast, it is imperative that we be constantly reminded of who we really are.

Using the guidelines the Torah spells out for the king won't make us into the modern equivalent of a prophet such as Shmuel or Yeshayahu. The king's rules were not designed for someone who is able to focus so forcefully on God, but rather for someone with situational impediments which prevent him from living such a life. They can only make us the modern equivalent of a King David, for example. Not bad, when you think about it. Not bad at all.

CHAPTER 6

Amalek versus Yehoshua

THE BIBLICALLY MANDATED vendetta against the nation of Amalek is well known to all religious Jews, enshrined as it is in a variety of rituals designed to keep its memory alive. Infamy notwithstanding, its roots are not so easily decipherable. In fact, its very existence is not without some serious questions.

As Netziv asks, why should God include this among His eternal commandments when its ultimate point, the eradication of Amalek, was basically accomplished a long time ago? Moreover, Netziv continues, even if there may be a few of Amalek's descendants still walking around, it is difficult to understand all the commotion about something that long ago stopped being any sort of threat whatsoever. Finally, he asks, if we are commanded to eradicate not only the renegade nation but its very memory, the Torah makes that impossible simply by mentioning it. And since the Torah is eternal and will always be read, says Netziv, it appears that we will always hear about Amalek, even after most other nations have long been forgotten![1]

The Torah has two main discussions about Amalek, the first in *Shemot* (17:8–16) and the second in *Devarim* (25:17–19). The first includes a longer discussion of Amalek's attack against the children of Israel on their way out from Egypt and God's subsequent command to wage perpetual war against this enemy. We are told of a formal battle led by Yehoshua and organized by

---

1   *Ha'amek Davar, Shemot* 17:14.

Moshe.[2] And while the passage in *Devarim* also summarizes this battle, it also adds strikingly new details. Abarbanel points out that a cursory reading makes it sound as if the Torah is describing an altogether different battle, telling us about a surprise attack against the stragglers in the Israelite camp.

Perhaps more difficult to understand is the role played by Yehoshua. In the passage in *Shemot*, he appears out of nowhere to become the head of the Jewish army. Even more curious is the Torah's insistence that his personal duty to fight against Amalek is to continue even after the war, such that God commands Moshe that the injunction to destroy Amalek be "placed in [Yehoshua's] ears."[3] To further complicate matters, he is called Yehoshua in this battle even though his name is formally changed from Hoshea to Yehoshua only later, in the story of the spies.[4] In short, Yehoshua dramatically appears on the scene, taking a major role in the conflict, and then goes right back into the shadows, appearing only occasionally throughout the rest of the Torah.[5]

A Nation of Pirates

Before we get back to the questions about the man who would become Moshe's successor, it might be helpful to address another question: From the text it is not so clear why such harsh treatment is reserved uniquely for Amalek.[6] Why is this nation considered worse than the Egyptians, who afflicted the Jews for hundreds of years, or even the Moabites, who used all sorts of machinations to destroy the Jews when they crossed the desert? The fact that quite a few answers are given demonstrates that there is no single, obvious answer.[7]

2   Abarbanel, *parashat Ki Tetzei*, question 26. Essentially, Abarbanel held there were two wars – or at least two battles – and that the passage in *Shemot* relates to both of them, whereas the passage in *Devarim* relates only to the first one.

3   *Shemot* 17:14.

4   *Bemidbar* 13:16.

5   Most notably in the story of the spies (*Bemidbar* 13:1–14:10), even though he is relatively quiet, and in passages that have to do with the succession of leadership in *Bemidbar* 27:18–22 and *Devarim* 31:3–23.

6   See Ramban, *Shemot* 17:16.

7   A good summary of the reasons generally given can be found in Abarbanel, *op. cit.*

The commandment in the book of *Devarim* to remember what Amalek did to the Jews gives some explanation as to what was most objectionable about that nation's behavior. The key verse tells us that Amalek "came (or chanced) upon you (the Israelites) in the desert and cut off your tail (*vayizanev*) – all of those who were struggling after you, and you were tired and exhausted – and did not fear God."[8] Commentators struggle with this verse for many reasons, not the least of which is that it is difficult to ascertain which part gives us the explanation we are looking for. Nor are all of its components clear in their own right.

The most intuitive issue presented by the Torah is that Amalek picked on those struggling to keep up with the march of the Jewish camp. For our purposes, we will assume that this is, in fact, the reason for our enmity. While the Torah's own laws of war[9] don't expressly forbid attacks on stragglers, it may be a case of something so obvious that the Torah did not feel the need to mandate it.[10] Moreover, the Torah makes provisions for non-combatants to escape.[11] But even if all of the above is true, why is attacking the enemy's weak elements so despicable that it warrants eternal enmity? It appears that the answer to that is in the last part of the verse: "and [they] did not fear God."

Attacking the helpless does not always come from the base immorality of those who don't fear God. Sometimes it is the only survival strategy of the weak, of those who simply don't have the power to engage more powerful opponents head-on. The Torah tells us this was not the case with Amalek, who were so strong that the Israelites required great effort to defeat them.[12] Their

---

8   *Devarim* 25:18. It is not clear whether the last part of the verse: "and did not fear God," is speaking about Amalek or about the Jewish stragglers, though the former would make more sense in context and we will follow that understanding here. It is also the favored approach among the classical commentators.

9   See Rambam, *Mishneh Torah, Hilchot Melachim* 6. See also Lawrence Schiffman and Joel B. Wolowelsky (eds.), *War and Peace in the Jewish Tradition* (New York: Yeshiva University Press, 2007), especially R. Michael Broyde, "Just Wars, Just Battles, and Just Conduct in Jewish Law," pp. 1–44.

10   Rabbi S.D. Luzzatto, *Vayikra* 24:10, gives this as the reason why blasphemy was not legislated until it was committed for the first time.

11   Rambam, *op. cit.*, 7.

12   *Shemot* 17:11–13. Accordingly, some understand the description of Amalek in

decision to prey on the weak, then, could have come only from a rank insouciance about the rules of fair play implicit in living in God's world. Perhaps we can understand, if not necessarily forgive, attacking the helpless as the last-ditch strategy of a weak nation. It is quite another thing, however, when it becomes standard operating procedure, as it apparently was with Amalek. That could only come from the absence of fear of God.

Indeed, the nation of Amalek would become known as the area's marauders.[13] They were not a military nation in the sense of ancient Sparta, interested in valiant acts of conquest. As we see from the book of *Shmuel,* theirs was a culture of finding the easiest way to acquire booty. They searched for vacuums of power and law enforcement which would enable them to help themselves to the possessions of others. In such a situation, the more ruthless one is, the more successful he is as well, because the greatest limit on the activity of such people is their own conscience.

Awe and Decency

The Torah wants us to understand that Amalek's pirate-like existence did not emerge as a fluke, but rather was deeply rooted in their approach to life more generally, i.e., in what the Torah calls "not fearing God." On the face of it this is a strange claim, for which pagan nations of the time could actually be described as God-fearing? And yet Amalek is the only one the Torah singles out as not fearing God. It is important to note that from among the few times the concept is mentioned in this form is when Avraham says Avimelech's country was devoid of the fear of God[14] and when Yosef, posing as an Egyptian, reassures his brothers that he fears God.[15] As these references are dealing with non-Jews, it appears that even if almost all of the nations of the time were

---

Bemidbar 24:20 as the "first among nations" as referring to their formidable military prowess.

13　See *I Shmuel* 30:1–3 and its treatment by Rabbi Ya'akov Medan, "Amalek" (http://etzion.org.il/en/amalek), section C.

14　*Bereshit* 20:11.

15　Ibid., 42:18.

idolatrous, there was nevertheless an expectation that they should be – and, in fact, often were – "God-fearing."

The word for God used in all three instances discussed above is *Elokim*, the generic name connoting both power and the notion of God as the universal Creator and ruler of the natural world. Fearing God, then, could more generally be thought of as fearing higher powers, and thus not necessarily presuppose monotheism. Instead, it is an attitude that comes from acknowledging something greater than men and their nations, something that by its very transcendence informs the human condition. That power (or powers) has a unique connection to human beings and therefore demands, whether explicitly or implicitly, a modicum of respect for other people who share this condition. We may want to refer to it as awe – a generic awe that leads to a certain basic decency. Certainly in the cases we have noted such an idea fits much better than the theologically charged notion that we usually associate with the fear of God.

When the Torah tells us that the nation of Amalek did not fear God, it is saying that they were unrestrained by *any* concept of a higher power and thus possessed an unusual lack of common decency. They were the most extreme manifestation of this attitude. Their pirate-like behavior reflects a lack of respect for man's uniqueness and ultimately for the power that stands behind it. No wonder, then, that the Jews are commanded to blot out Amalek. They represent an antithesis to the Jewish nation's mission in the world, and their approach to life presents a formidable obstacle to the Jewish people's goal of establishing a kingdom of God on earth.

The fight against Amalek does not end when the nation is destroyed, for even when it would be defeated its legacy would likely remain. As long as greed exists in the human heart, there will always be a need to fight against the temptation to view others as mere objects standing in the way of one's advancement.[16] The eternal struggle against Amalek is how Judaism formalizes this need.[17]

---

16 This is one of the main themes in *Crime and Punishment*, by the Russian Christian writer Fyodor Dostoyevsky.

17 While Netziv (*Ha'amek Davar, Shemot* 17:14) presents a different approach, he also

Amalek and Atrocity

The lack of awe we just described may have led, and historically has often led, to something even more problematic than the objectification of others. A closer reading of the text opens up such an understanding here as well.

There is a very unusual verb describing what Amalek did to the Jews, *vayizanev*. While it is not clear exactly what it means, the root *zanav*, tail, gives us a good clue. Most commentators understand the use of this root in context to mean, as mentioned earlier, that Amalek attacked the stragglers at the back of the Israelite camp.[18] But there is another understanding offered in the Midrash[19] and subsequently by Rashi.[20] The tail that was acted upon doesn't relate to the Israelite camp but to another appendage of individual Israelite soldiers. Accordingly, this approach to the text tells us that Amalek castrated the Jews they attacked in order to show their disdain for their victims.

The Midrash connects this with the mitzva of circumcision and the possibility that Amalek's sudden and strange attack on the Israelites may have been more than a routine assault to obtain plunder. It was an expression of utter contempt for God's Torah and its commandments. Mangling the human organ of circumcision was Amalek's way of showing this.

Since it is hard (though obviously, not impossible) to imagine such a scenario on a purely literal level, the rabbis may actually have been referring to the existential opposition that existed between Amalek's national character and God's general mandate to the Jews, which is at least partly represented by circumcision. Even if the historical Amalek did not know enough about the Jews or their Torah to plan how to agitate against them, their very behavior was in itself an affront to that which the Torah stood for.[21] The Torah is meant to bring a God-consciousness into the world, ideally by encouraging

---

posits that it is not the nation of Amalek that we need to perpetually blot out but rather their attitude and ideology.

18 Ibn Ezra, *Devarim* 25:18. See also Radak, *Yehoshua* 10:19.

19 *Tanchuma, Ki Tetzei* 10.

20 Rashi, *Devarim* 25:18.

21 In my upcoming volume on *Vayikra*, I will discuss why this commandment was especially antithetical to the Amalekite ethos.

compassion toward His creatures but at the very least by demanding a basic decency toward them. Amalek's attitude toward others shows an attitude that can only push God-consciousness away from mankind.

On a simple textual level, it is likely that mutilating the bodies of their enemies was standard practice for Amalek, done as a matter of policy. And it reflects even more strongly their lack of fear of God. Where there is no reverence, there are no limits. In such a situation, what ultimately results is a state that Hobbes famously describes as "nasty and brutish." In fact, there can be no better description of Amalek's modus vivendi in its struggle against Israel.

Amalek and Esav

Because Amalek represents the antithesis of Judaism, Jewish tradition shows great interest in this otherwise insignificant nation. For one, it looks at Amalek's antecedents in order to understand how people can turn into monsters. The roots of the Amalekites are fairly well known: the Torah tells us the people are named after a grandson of Esav.[22] Jewish tradition supplements this information by describing Amalek as the most antagonistic of Esav's progeny.[23]

Amalek himself notwithstanding, it is almost expected that a descendent of Esav would be in conflict with the descendants of Ya'akov. For even if there was an apparently peaceful reconciliation between Ya'akov and Esav back in *Bereshit*,[24] the story is nuanced enough to leave several rabbinic voices wondering whether Esav's descendants can be trusted. Likewise, we continue to wonder whether there would have been continued resentment with regard to the blessing and birthright that Esav lost to Ya'akov and his descendants.[25]

Some commentators suggest that Amalek's struggle against Israel is a continuation of the vendetta between the two brothers. This serves as the prime

---

22 *Bereshit* 6:12. See also, Rabbi Y.S. Reggio, *Shemot* 17:8, who presents solid evidence that this grandson was actually the leader of the nation at the time of the attack on the Jews on their way out of Egypt.

23 See, for example, *Tanchuma, Shelach* 9.

24 *Bereshit* 33:1–17.

25 See *Sifrei, Beha'alotecha* 69.

motivation for Amalek's otherwise difficult to understand attack against Israel.[26] In this context, it is important to recall that the blessing Yitzchak gives Esav and his descendants makes their success seemingly contingent on the failure of Ya'akov's descendants.[27] Hence, to the extent that the nation of Amalek was aware of this, its members would certainly have had an interest in destroying the new Jewish nation – and to do so at this point, before it became more settled and powerful.

Part of the suspicion surrounding Esav's continued hatred of Ya'akov, however, comes not from the issue of unfinished business as much as from the personality traits the rabbis saw in Esav. Some readers miss why rabbinic tradition seems so stacked against Esav, especially in view of his being taken advantage of by his younger brother. But while the difficulties Esav faced may partially excuse his problematic behavior, Yitzchak's blessing that he should live by the sword did not come out of the blue. He was already known as the hunter of the family.[28] This in itself need not be a bad thing. Violence against animals and even people has its place in the context of human survival and prosperity. That being said, it is also easily misused.

And so it is with Esav. He is the first person in the Bible who threatens to kill someone, and not just a random someone but his own brother.[29] Although we see fratricide with the Bible's very first brothers, Kayin's murder of Hevel was not premeditated and it was apparently regretted. Moreover, its shadows do not cast the same pallor on future events that would be the case with Esav's behavior.

A careful reading of Esav's story shows many other deficiencies in his personality,[30] but even if all we had to go on was his stated intention to murder

---

26 Foremost being Abarbanel, *Shemot* 17:8. See also Malbim ad loc. Amos Chacham, in his commentary in *Da'at Mikra*, tries to find a more rational explanation for the attack. In spite of his best efforts, however, there seems to be no hint to these reasons in the Torah itself.

27 *Bereshit* 27:40.

28 Ibid., 25:27.

29 Ibid., 27:41.

30 See, for example, ibid., 26:34–5, where his choice of wives meets the clear disapproval of his parents. Moreover, his disdain for his own birthright (ibid., 25:34) is also commonly understood to show poor character.

his brother, that would be enough in order to understand him as someone who sees others as mere objects. One who is prepared to murder another human being is showing that another's right to life is purely dependent upon the aggressor's own needs or preferences – similar to how most of us think about inanimate objects.

Of all of Esav's descendants, we only see Amalek taking on this trait of nonchalance toward the sanctity of life that most rational human beings find so objectionable. While rapprochement with the other descendants of Esav is at least a possibility,[31] the Torah seems to rule it out when it comes to Amalek.

Yehoshua and Yosef

It is not only on Amalek's side that there is a connection to earlier generations; it appears to be relevant on the Jewish side of the battle lines as well. Earlier, we mentioned the very strong but far from obvious connection between Yehoshua and the war with Amalek. The Midrash offers several explanations for this, most of them based on Yehoshua's being descended from Yosef.[32] There is a strong tradition that the nemesis of Amalek's ancestor Esav is none other than Yehoshua's ancestor Yosef. We could conclude, therefore, that Yehoshua is chosen for this fight by virtue of his ancestry.

But going back a step we need to ask the question: what is it about Yosef that made him a thorn in Esav's side? Most of the midrashic literature cites various contrasting parallels that make them appear to be polar opposites. For example, Esav loses his birthright to his younger brother and Yosef acquires some firstborn rights from his older brother.[33] In general, the various contrasts point to Esav's succumbing when faced by moral challenges, while Yosef does not. Furthermore, the Midrash points out that in order to vanquish the powerful Esav, it was necessary for Yosef to have lived a life that would bring an especially high level of Divine favor.

---

31 See *Redeeming Relevance in Genesis*, Chapter 5.
32 *Shemot Rabba* 26:3.
33 See *Bereshit Rabba* 99:2 and especially *Pesikta Rabbati* 12:5–6, both of which list several other examples.

A closer look at the relevant midrashic literature shows that Yosef actually had a lot in common with Esav. This is so much the case that we could even construe Esav to be his alter ego. For example, the rabbis note that just as Esav did not learn from the two righteous men who surrounded him (Yitzchak and Ya'akov), Yosef did not learn from the two evildoers who surrounded him (Potiphar and Pharaoh).[34] One could say that this too emphasizes their dissimilarity, but in fact we see that they were both too strong-willed to be affected by their surroundings. Moreover, returning to the previous example, although one gained the leadership associated with the firstborn and the other one lost it,[35] it was clearly of great importance to both of them. And the importance they both attached to it may have had a great deal to do with their aspirations of inheriting their respective fathers' legacies. In this regard, something the Midrash doesn't mention is that both were their respective fathers' favorites.[36] They both also understood that their fathers' favor would be a major weapon in inheriting both the legacy and the leadership. All of this, then, fits into a general personality type – one that is characterized by strong will and a natural attraction to leadership.

Having a very strong will makes it more difficult for an individual not to claim more rights and privileges than the others surrounding him would. This attitude isn't engendered merely out of a sense of entitlement; it also stems from a feeling that as a natural born leader he can do more with human and

34 *Pesikta Rabbati*, ibid.

35 Even if Esav appears to have given his birthright away to Ya'akov without much resistance, the incident remained a sore spot for him, as we see when the blessing is taken away later on (*Bereshit* 27:36). Moreover, Esav's concern with the blessing and its legacy may also have gone above and beyond those aspects of the birthright he gave away, as per *Bereshit Rabba* 63:13, which is subsequently cited by Rashi, *Bereshit* 25:31.

36 The *Pesikta Rabbati* cited above (notes 33 and 34) does not examine Yosef's and Esav's relationship with their fathers as much as the unusual relationship each had with his mother. Yosef protected his mother from Esav's potential sexual advance and Esav, according to this Midrash, wanted to kill his mother. In both cases one need not subscribe to Freudian psychology to note the complicated involvement each had with their mothers. In any event, perhaps their very strength of character is what makes them go beyond the parameters of the more typical mother-child relationship.

material resources than others. There is ample room here to say that we are dealing with the temptation of such a personality to claim the Nietzschean prerogative to that which his superior nature "entitles" him. For Esav this translates into a right to kill his brother when the latter gets in the way of his plans. It also translates into choosing multiple wives in a household where this is not the norm. Furthermore, given Esav's clear interest in pleasing his father, choosing wives of whom he knew his father would disapprove could only have come from a sense that he absolutely needed them to suit himself and satisfy his desires.

It is evident that Yosef also had a very strong will. Accordingly, when the rabbis tell us that Yosef did not give in to sexual immorality, they elaborate on how difficult it was for him to resist the allures of Potiphar's wife.[37] The situation would have made this a challenge for anyone, but it appears from the Midrash that Yosef's personality may have made it even harder still. And although Yosef's inclination to murder is not as obvious, his relish for power and control is apparent to all. Besides recounting his dreams, when he finally attains power over his brothers in Egypt, the ease with which he manipulates them shows a sense of entitlement that allows him to play with the lives of others – something which is theoretically only a few steps removed from premeditated murder.

In light of the rabbinic literature we have just explored, it is now easier for us to comprehend how Yosef's ability to confront Esav stems from the former's ability to understand the latter. It also illustrates the tremendous willpower required to take on a competitor equally determined to come out on top.

With this in mind, we can understand an otherwise difficult statement of the rabbis chastising Yosef for telling Pharaoh's wine steward to speak well of him to Pharaoh.[38] Ostensibly, Yosef was simply doing what was expected and using all the means at his disposal to ameliorate his situation. The problem instead lay in how Yosef framed the situation. What was he thinking when he asked the steward to remember him to Pharaoh? It is clear that if he could claim a favor from Pharaoh's servant, the latter would simply become a ticket

37 See *Sotah* 36b.
38 *Bereshit Rabba* 89:3.

out of jail. In fact, there is no indication that Yosef was thinking anything else when he asked him to speak to Pharaoh.

Had Yosef actually been concerned about the well-being of his cellmates, his behavior might have been quite different. For instance, would he have told the head baker about his disastrous fate so readily? At the very least, would he not have offered him some comfort? With regard to the wine steward, then, the rabbis seem to be troubled by Yosef objectifying him. And that is precisely the issue at the heart of the Amalekite perspective.

The characteristics Yosef and Esav share require great discipline and self-control. The interface between Israel and Amalek is ultimately between one who manages to control his negative impulses and one who does not. So while Yosef admittedly had these tendencies and their accompanying challenges, he was ultimately able to remake himself into the righteous leader that forgave and comforted his brothers. According to the rabbis, in the end, only a man who can work up the same type of self-concerned hatred as Esav and nevertheless subdue his impulses can stand up to an Esav. Such a man would confront his adversary by saying, "I understand you. I know what you're feeling. But acting upon that feeling only happens because you don't see that others also exist – and that they exist not only for your benefit." It is such a personality that will ultimately stop an Esav bent on violent revenge.

Yosef himself was unable to develop the complete self-control needed to finally defeat Esav. The perfection of this trait would be realized only with his descendants, perhaps starting with Yehoshua. Conversely, the lack of self-control in the face of ego would not be fully realized with Esav. That would happen only with his descendant Amalek. When Yehoshua fought against Amalek, it represented a second and not completely conclusive round. The final round will apparently occur only far in the future, in messianic times.[39]

Amalek and Yosef

The Midrash mentioned earlier asking why Yehoshua should be the one to fight Amalek makes a linguistic connection between Yehoshua's ancestor

39 *Ovadia* 1:15–21.

Yosef's proclamation that he feared God and the description of Amalek as not fearing God. Though the connection need not be more than linguistic, Rabbi Baruch Epstein presents a deeper notion very much in consonance with our understanding. He points out that when Yosef said he feared God, he said it as an Egyptian, not as a Jew. He was proclaiming that such an attitude is expected from Jew and non-Jew alike.[40] Only someone who speaks about what is expected from everyone, and who lives by it, can impose it on others.

Hence the connection between Yosef on the one hand and Esav and his descendants on the other does not only involve a question of understanding similar strong-willed personalities, it also involves Yosef's particular interest in universal morality. As a benevolent viceroy in Egypt, it is he who designed the model of a Jewish leader in a foreign land, one who tries to promote a more moral vision for all mankind.[41] And since Amalek represents a moral threat to the gentiles – who are more susceptible to his influence – even more than he does to the Jews, he would be of particular interest to Yosef.

The moral fear of God broadcast by Yosef is universal. Nevertheless, it can be seen as part of the Jewish mission. Although Yosef predated the actual establishment of the Jewish nation, it was he who proclaimed fear of God to the world. Likewise, in the fight of all decent people against Amalek, it would be a Jew and a descendant of Yosef who would need to continue to proclaim it to the world – this time not with words but with actions.

Yehoshua the Conqueror

The previous section sought to explain Yehoshua's involvement with Amalek based on his past, i.e., his ancestry. But the most immediate reason Yehoshua needed to know about Amalek has more to do with his future than his past. Upon entering the land, Yehoshua (and specifically carrying the name Yehoshua and not his previous name, Hoshea) would be leading many battles,

---

40 *Torah Temimah, Shemot* 17, note 5.
41 See, for example, the famous Midrash (*Tanchuma, Miketz* 7) wherein Yosef orders the Egyptians to circumcise themselves.

both great and small. Among the battles that presumably lay ahead was that against Amalek. Furthermore, beyond that specific battle, it appears that there was something more general in the struggle against Amalek that Yehoshua needed to apply to the conquest of all of Canaan.

Lest one object that at the time of the war against Amalek recorded in the Torah, when Yehoshua was designated to continue the struggle against Amalek, it had not yet been decreed that Yehoshua would lead the Jews into the Land of Israel, the rabbis have already pointed out that God's omniscience forced His own hand here. Out of the need to prepare the Jews for dealing with Amalek, He gave them the first inkling of Yehoshua's eventual succession of Moshe.[42] It was probably not even noticed at the time. Yet in hindsight, it was critical for the future conqueror to connect to this experience in real time.

The lessons of Amalek represent a very important warning to any Jewish military leader, Yehoshua being only the first. It is easy to uphold the highest standards of war during peacetime, but it is quite another for them to be upheld by a desperate general whose only chance to win lies in his willingness to fight a dirty war. Even a general who is not so desperate will sometimes be tempted to cut corners.

Everyone knows that war is a nasty business, and it is difficult to imagine that morality and rules have any place in it. Yet even in the midst of the horrors of war, the Torah maintains that there is a need to maintain a basic respect for what it means to be human. This translates into a code of behavior that tells us that expediency is not everything, even when dealing with mortal enemies. Many niceties that exist in peacetime are placed to the side, and a thinner, emergency-footing morality sets in, but this is very different from the waiving of morality altogether.

As Israel's first true military leader, it was essential for Yehoshua to understand Amalek as the anti-model. After all, we learn from our competitors. Amalek proved to be the most effective of all the armies that Israel would encounter on the way to its land.[43] There is no doubt, then, of the temptation to learn how war should be fought specifically from them.

42 *Tanchuma, Beshalach* 28.
43 In this regard, also see ibid., *Chukat* 18.

Amalek's example is particularly enticing for someone descended from Yosef. In fact, many of his later descendants who ruled the northern kingdom of Israel would live by the notion that the ends justify the means. In such governance, everything is subordinated to the success of the state. If the leaders of the northern kingdom did not exactly stoop to the depths of Amalek, the road they traveled had many similarities.

For several reasons, then, we can understand God's unique and emphatic language when instructing Moshe to communicate Amalek's derelict status to his eventual successor: "Place it into the ears of Yehoshua."[44] It is apparently not enough for Yehoshua to merely be told about it. He needs to internalize it; it has to go *into* his ears. Below, we will see just how important this would be.

The Ultimate Cutting of Tails

The final link in the story of Yehoshua and Amalek is very subtle. The uncommon verb based on the Hebrew word for tail that we discussed above is repeated only once more in the entire Tanach, specifically from the mouth of Yehoshua.[45]

Five powerful kings have arrayed themselves to fight against the Jews in order to forestall the latter's imminent conquest of their lands. But rather than fight Yehoshua's army they pick on his weak ally, the Giv'onim (Gibeonites). In response to his helpless allies' cry of distress, Yehoshua gives his strange command. He stops the sun, then orders his own troops, *"vezinavtem otam,"* which is usually understood to mean they should chase their enemies.

As we learned, however, the verb more specifically denotes either an attack on a camp's rear guard or the act of castration. This might lead one to think that in spite of the precautions taken by God and by Moshe, Yosef's warrior descendant was simply unable to overcome this difficult temptation. Given

---

44 In Chapter Eight we discuss a very similar expression, "to place words into someone's mouth" (see pp. 110–111). Much of what we say there applies here as well.
45 *Yehoshua* 10:19.

the lowly stature of his opponents, it would have been tempting to forget about the Divine image that existed even in these despicable enemies.

Thankfully, this reading lacks evidence in both text and tradition. Moreover, the use of the root *z-n-v* seems to go virtually unnoticed, as if the command *vezinavtem* were just another tactic of war. Yet the word was chosen specifically in these two contexts and nowhere else in all of Tanach, which indicates that something is being communicated to the attentive reader.

Perhaps one can understand the tie-in in a different fashion: That what God and Moshe were teaching Yehoshua from the initial battle with Amalek is that there are two types of nations. Most nations (one hopes) live with at least a modicum of fear of God, and thus this is the default. The laws of war apply to those nations because fear of God represents a minimal internalization of what it means to be human. Relations with such nations are determined by many things, but their annihilation is simply not an option.

Not so, however, with nations such as Amalek, who have forfeited being considered created in the image of God. And those concerning whom Yehoshua commands his troops to "cut off their tails" seem to have a definite Amalekite character. They were behaving like Amalek, essentially showing that they lacked the fear of God and thus thought of other humans beings as mere objects – made, like beasts, for human use. At that point Yehoshua tells his troops to treat this particular opponent the way it would treat others – no differently from beasts.

* * *

The scary thing about Amalek is that he is human. Moreover, given the many atrocities committed throughout history, we see that the path of Amalek is *uniquely* human, displaying behavior that we see from no other living creature. It shows the alter ego of our unique Divine image and our complete freedom to choose even the most despicable actions. Yet as we have discussed, the story of Amalek and his spiritual descendants is also the story of those who completely deny their Divine image. The Torah wants us to be quite clear of that.

We have seen that even being Jewish does not immunize us from following in Amalek's footsteps. Not only does a leader such as Yehoshua need to be prevented from emulating Amalek, proper conduct in wartime had to be *pushed* onto him. If someone as great as he needed to be inoculated from sinking to the depths of an Amalek, we can only assume that the way of this quintessential enemy of Judaism is not completely foreign to us either. As important as the perpetual vigil against the outer Amalek may be, the vigil against the inner Amalek may be more important still.

CHAPTER 7

The Final Commandments

B Y NOW WE have seen many facets of the book of *Devarim*, but we have yet to discuss a way to tie all these various strands together. A more concerted look at the book's legal corpus will help us in this regard. For if *Mishneh Torah* really means "a second law," we would expect this body of laws to somehow convey *Devarim*'s essence. Giving the legal section pride of place in the middle of the book[1] fosters that impression as well.

Understanding how these laws go to the core of the book is no easy task, however.[2] Examining *Devarim*'s laws, we often go from one to another without any sense of what they have in common. But although it is not always clear how the various laws were organized, it is quite evident that their order is not random.

One place where a pattern is more obvious is at the end of Devarim's legal section, where we find its last three eternal laws (as opposed to one-time, historical injunctions, such as the ceremony to hear the blessings and the curses[3]). Not only is its content interrelated, its format is particularly informative as well. And if we narrow our focus even further, to the last two laws, we encounter formulaic declarations that seem to carry much more meaning than the actual commandments with which these declarations are connected. Furthermore, this section takes us a long way toward understanding

---

1   Chapters 12–26.
2   See Chapter Two, where we discuss which laws were and were not included in this book and why.
3   *Devarim* 27:11–26.

what *Devarim* is ultimately all about. In fact, the Torah's final three laws – the eradication of Amalek, the obligation to bring the firstfruits (*bikkurim*), and the declaration concerning the disposal of one's tithes (*vidui ma'aser*)[4] – can be understood as a general summary of the entire Torah. More on this below.

Even a casual reader may notice that there is something special about the Torah's final commandments. Starting from the middle of the trio, we find the well-known declaration that begins with the elusive phrase, *Arami oved avi*, generally translated either as "my father was a lost Aramean"[5] or "an Aramean [tried to] destroy my father."[6] As with the *Shema* passage, this declaration became enshrined in the liturgy (specifically in the Haggadah), and as a result has taken on an important place in the Jewish consciousness. But even if this passage had not been included in our liturgy, it represents an unusually neat summary of the core of early Jewish history. Nestled between the injunction to remember Amalek and the declaration of having properly given tithes, it goes right to the heart of the Jewish experience. Let us briefly examine its connection to and enhancement by the two commandments that surround it.

Amalek and *Bikkurim*

Many commentators remark that the placement of the *bikkurim* declaration right after the injunction to destroy Amalek is significant. For example, Abarbanel writes how the Jews' difficult war with Amalek contrasts with the main historical experience of Divine salvation recounted in the *bikkurim* declaration. He goes on to say that the rabbinic authorities who determined how to divide up the weekly Torah readings separated these two laws specifically to distinguish between "the light and the darkness." He then rejects the opinion of Ibn Ezra, who understands the placement of these laws in separate sections to mean that after the Jews are settled in their land and need to destroy Amalek as the next step, they are also to remember that there are other things (i.e., *bikkurim*) that should have already been done.[7]

4   Ibid., 25:17–18, 26:1–11 and 26:12–15, respectively.
5   Rashi, *Devarim* 26:5.
6   Rashbam, Ibn Ezra, ibid.
7   Abarbanel, *Devarim* 26:1.

Perhaps the most creative suggestion is that of Malbim, who reminds us that Amalek is a descendent of Esav and thus remains in conflict with Ya'akov due to the latter's taking Esav's firstborn status away from him. Malbim points out that the command that follows the one to destroy Amalek hints to its being the source of Amalek's hate for Israel, as the word for firstborn privileges, *bechora*, is both conceptually and linguistically related to *bikkurim*, the word for firstfruits.[8]

The fact that so many commentators seek a connection between the first two commandments in the trio points to there being something intuitive about the connection – even if its content is somewhat elusive. Abarbanel's explanation strikes us as the closest. In his distinguishing between two fundamental historical experiences, we can see the Torah trying to present some sort of cumulative summary. There is likewise room to see that after being given these commandments, the Jews must also take the essence of their mission with them as well. Similar to the contrast between the light and darkness of the historical experience, one could divide their mission in a way that could be summarized as *sur me'ra va'aseh tov* (turn away from evil and do good).[9]

One might be tempted to dismiss this one-line summary of how to relate to good and evil as overly obvious. But as with many other things we have seen so far, the genius may be found more in the delivery than in the content. For just to read about good and evil is far from enough – mere words, no matter how strong or profound, rarely motivate people. Instead, this most important charge must be couched in a story in order to make it resonate with each individual Jew. The injunction to blot out Amalek is telling the Jews to destroy evil while remembering the bitterness they experienced so harshly via the barbaric assault on their stragglers by their nemesis. The Israelites likely saw that fierce and wanton attack as the epitome of evil, the roots of which they would

---

8   Malbim, *Devarim* 25:18, end. Though Malbim doesn't say it, one could develop this idea further and suggest that the *bikkurim* actually serve as a type of atonement for the Jewish people's acquisition of the *bechora* under questionable circumstances. Their willingness to sacrifice *bikkurim* to a higher purpose and not to use them for personal enjoyment serves as a symbolic declaration that they will not derive any national benefit from the *bechora*.

9   *Tehillim* 34:15.

viscerally want to destroy. Through this, the basic concept of eradicating evil would be forever cemented within the Jewish national consciousness.

As per our adaptation of Abarbanel, the second part of the Jewish mission is to do good. Here too, it would not be enough to simply say, "Do good." There would need to be some sort of model of the good with which the Jews were tremendously impressed – so much so that they would want to emulate it. They did not have far to look. God had taken the small family of Ya'akov with which the Jews began, nurtured it and favored it against overwhelming odds, and ultimately gave it a land full of unsurpassed bounty. As with the immediate repulsion that the Jews would feel when remembering the actions of Amalek, likewise would they immediately and overwhelmingly feel a sense of gratitude when remembering all the kindnesses shown them by God. Just as the commandment to wipe out Amalek is actually a stand-in for all the commandments of "turn away from evil," so too, the firstfruits are meant to represent all commandments that could be summarized by the phrase, "Do good."

Bikkurim and Ma'aser

The "doing good" symbolized by the firstfruits is not the last commandment of the trio – which it might very well have been if it were the end of the Jewish mission. The last commandment, the declaration concerning tithes, takes the idea of the firstfruits one step further. It tells us that the feeling engendered by bringing one's firstfruits is not meant to end there, but rather – and this is what the commandment of tithes is all about – to give to others, and spread good further. Jews are taught not just to admire but to imitate the God Who had been so munificent toward them. In these specific circumstances it would mean giving tithes fully and ungrudgingly, but in the larger picture it should be taken as the charge to act with kindness and generosity in all circumstances.

As pointed out by many, the phrase that appears most in the *bikkurim* section is that of what God has given (*natan*) to the Jewish people.[10] Although

---

10 See Martin Buber, "The Prayer of the First Fruits," in *On the Bible: Eighteen Studies* (Syracuse: Syracuse University Press, 1982), p. 125, who is subsequently cited by R.

generally overlooked, the same theme is also used repeatedly in the subsequent passage discussing man's gifts to his fellow. In the context of the spiritual challenges posed by bounty, this type of awareness is extremely important. By being reminded of where bounty comes from and being instructed on how to look at his national past, the Jew is helped in accomplishing the Torah's elusive goal of "serving God in joy."[11] Such a goal includes the practical outcome of emulating God in this context: Just as He Who has everything gives of that which belongs to Him, so too, when we have much we should also give to others.

This is precisely what makes the declaration concerning tithes so central. The illusion of security brought about by wealth allows one to forget how precarious his existence is, and consequently to simply ignore his obligations to God and to his fellow man. The Torah thus warns that if we cannot remember to serve God when times are good, His only recourse is to take away those good times in order that we will feel we really "need" Him.[12] The sort of vicious cycle which forces God's hand to punish the Jews and elicit a "no atheist in a foxhole" response is exactly what the internalization of the *bikkurim* declaration is supposed to prevent.

Of Screams, Primal and Otherwise

Let us now return to the periscopic declaration made at the *bikkurim* rite. Besides the obvious theme of God's kindness to the Jews, something else stands out: The centrality of the Egyptian experience is boiled down to its spiritual essence. It begins with Ya'akov and his family going down to Egypt – with no mention of God.[13] However, as soon as things get really bad, the children of Israel bring Him into their lives. And they do so in a highly intense way, by

Elchanan Samet in *Torah MiEtzion, Devarim* (Jerusalem: Maggid Press, 2012), p. 310. See also *Recalling the Covenant*, p. 983, note 2, concerning the final use of this verb in the adjacent section on *vidui ma'aser*.

11 *Devarim* 28:47.

12 Ibid., verses 45–48.

13 Ibid., 26:5.

"crying out to Him."[14] Only then does the Torah describe God as hearing and seeing the plight of His people. Jewish tradition, as well as most other theistic conceptions of God, cannot accept the literal implication of this, i.e., that God is not always aware of what is happening to people. But for all human purposes (according to which the Torah is written[15]), if God doesn't overtly react to the oppression of innocents, it is as if He is not hearing and not seeing. We certainly want God to "hear and see" us, and hear and see us He does – but only after the children of Israel initiate the connection by their action of crying out to Him. This is a central lesson of the Egyptian experience: we can bring about Divine involvement only if we elicit it.

Evoking God's involvement is not always easy. What is implied in the above retelling (and also in its initial rendition in *Shemot*[16]) is that it is not enough to pray or to make declarations. Rather, one has to cry out with a high level of intensity. We all know that conjuring this up when times are good can be quite difficult. Constantly reminding ourselves of the need to connect to God through the *bikkurim* declaration might not be enough to engender the required intensity, but at least it gives us a chance to quickly and simply reflect on our dependence on God in a significant way.

The *bikkurim* declaration doesn't bring just an idea to our attention however. The Torah doesn't call upon the Jew to merely meditate on the need to be grateful to God; he has to truly *speak* about it. And lest he conjure up listless recitals of the American Pledge of Allegiance, the Torah uses the word *ve'anita* ("answer") instead of the word *ve'amarta* ("say"). According to Jewish tradition, and posited by many commentators as well, *ve'anita* means to respond in a loud voice.[17] In particular, according to Rabbi Y.S. Reggio, the word really indicates loud song.[18]

As opposed to simply raising one's voice, then, one actively seeks to access emotion. And emotion here is actually the whole point. Be it the emotion of thanksgiving as with the firstfruits, or the emotion of desperation with regard

---

14 Ibid., verses 6–7.
15 See *Redeeming Relevance in Exodus*, pp. 15–20.
16 *Shemot* 1–2.
17 *Sotah* 32a; Rashi, *Devarim* 26:5.
18 Rabbi Y.S. Reggio, *Devarim*, ibid.

to Egyptian oppression, the Jew will be successful in his relationship with God only if he pursues it from the depths of his heart.

When the Jew performed the *bikkurim* ritual, speaking about his ancestors crying out to God, he himself was speaking loudly, thereby *reenacting the experience* rather than just telling it over. And even if his cry was a joyful one and therefore not in line with the cry of his forebears, both represent true engagement of the heart.

Although the *bikkurim* ritual was focused on times of bounty, the Jewish people took the idea even further, understanding the centrality of the message for bad times as well as for good. As a result, they incorporated this passage, if not necessarily its complete performance, into the Haggadah text, which has been used from the earliest Roman oppression and throughout the long Exile that ensued.

History, Torah and Relationship

Obviously, any five-and-a-half-verse summary of several centuries of Jewish history cannot include all of the most important events, let alone those of lesser importance. Still, we would be remiss if we didn't look more carefully at what is being excluded here. Rabbi Moshe Shamah brings up the most glaring omission, the revelation at Mount Sinai, which is not even hinted to in this summary. His answer that the farmer's gratitude for his land makes it superfluous[19] may well be true, but it requires further explanation. Given that this is not only a declaration for the farmer but one that would designedly take a central role as *the* declaration of Jewish history, the question takes on more urgency.

While it is the subject of another and longer discussion, we must remember that some of the Bible's greatest heroes lived before the Torah was given. This did not prevent them from living exemplary lives and from connecting with God via sublime prophecy and prayer. The constant for the Jews who lived in the era covered by the *bikkurim* declaration, i.e., from Ya'akov's going

19 *Recalling the Covenant*, p. 981.

down to Egypt until and including Egyptian oppression, is the striving to attain an ethical and spiritual lifestyle, the tools for which do not have to be based on the Torah *per se*. Hence it would be an error to see the revelation at Sinai as a complete game changer. As central as the Torah is to Judaism, it remains a means and not an end in itself. Granted, the only way a Jew can ideally fulfill his role in life is by following the precepts of the Torah. His actual goal, however, remains living that role, which the Torah but helps him fulfill.

On some level, the point of man's existence can be boiled down to one idea, and that is positive involvement with God.[20] Accordingly, the history of the Jewish people is more about relationship than it is about the Torah or about any particular story. Relationship primarily consists of communication, which by its very nature goes in both directions. At Sinai the Jews likely heard God more clearly than at any other point in history, but God did not hear the Jews. This is not to take anything away from *Ma'amad Har Sinai*. As we discussed in Chapter Three, the atmosphere was meant to be one of fear and trepidation and so communication was not supposed to be going in two directions.[21] Had the Jews also been enraptured in prayer, it would have taken away from what that event was all about.

Instead of *Ma'amad Har Sinai*, it is the Jews' crying out about their dismal condition in Egypt and God's long-term response to it – which doesn't end until He brings them to the Land of Israel at the conclusion of the book of Devarim – that ends up being the most emblematic of the Jewish people's involvement with God. And that is why it is the crux of the recitation here.

The giving of the Torah may still have been the single most important event in the history of the Jewish people, but that doesn't mean it had to be included in the *bikkurim* declaration. The declaration's being a historical summary notwithstanding, its point is not history. Its point is to instill a burning desire to do the right thing. Just as the Talmud points out that it is very difficult to hear two voices at the same time,[22] so too is it difficult to understand

---

20 See *Makkot* 24a, where two suggestions are given for the one idea that summarizes the entire Torah. Both suggestions (*Amos* 5:4; *Chavakkuk* 5:4) relate to the relationship between man and God.

21 Pp. 47–49.

22 *Megilla* 21b.

two messages at the same time. The idea of summarizing history here is to boil it down to a single message and nothing else.

* * *

In our spiritual lives it is not uncommon to feel that God is not answering us. An adult student once asked about that during a class I was giving, whereupon another student asked her whether she had ever truly prayed. The members of this class were people who all prayed on a daily basis. But the second student had actually made an extremely incisive point! How many of us can say that we have really and truly prayed with the intensity of the Jews in Egypt?

Part of our spiritual quest is to make our connection with God real even when we don't feel motivated. Indeed, the Torah's many laws attempt to deal with this problem by legislating all sorts of rituals and remembrances aimed at focusing our attention on that which should always be at the center of our lives, but generally is not – namely, our relationship with God.

It behooves us to go the extra mile and seek out ways of creating intense communion with God. As with the *bikkurim* declaration, it need not be something we do every day, but it must take place at regular intervals. Some people make regular pilgrimages to the Kotel in Jerusalem for precisely this reason. Others make a pilgrimage to the grave of R. Nachman of Breslav at Rosh Hashanah. They feel the experience of praying there with so many others on that auspicious day is enough to inspire them for the rest of the year.

These are only two examples of what can be done, and there are many others. Whatever we do, however, it is critical that we understand that we must constantly strive to be in communication with God. For if these last three laws of the Torah which we have just discussed were seen to be a summary of how the Torah wants us to act, their centerpiece, the *bikkurim* declaration, reminds us of what the Torah is ultimately all about.

CHAPTER 8

The Bittersweet Song

IN SEVERAL OF the preceding chapters, we have seen summary statements of Judaism recited on a regular basis – most prominently, the *Shema* passages and the *bikkurim* declaration. As we come to the end of the book of *Devarim* we find another variation on this theme, the song known by its first word, *Ha'azinu*.[1] Though we have no record of stated times for its recital by the entire people, the Talmud informs us that it was recited by the Levites in the Temple every Shabbat morning.[2]

This section, however, stands apart from the others in even more fundamental ways. It is dissimilar in style, content and even purpose. Moreover, we immediately note an unusual expression instructing Moshe "to place it in the mouths of *Bnei Yisrael*."[3] It is clear that Moshe is not being told to just teach

---

1   *Devarim* 32:1 ff.

2   *Rosh Hashanah* 31a. There Abbaye tells us that the reading was divided into six parts which would be recited on a rotating basis at the time of the *musaf*, the additional Shabbat offering.

3   Rashi, Ramban, *Devarim* 31:19. It is worth noting, however, that several commentators understand that it is not only *Ha'azinu* that is being described as a song here, but the entire Torah as well. See, for example, Ralbag and Rabbi S.R. Hirsch ad loc. Even though the Torah doesn't consistently contain the various features that are characteristic of song, still, as mentioned earlier, Netziv points out in his introduction to *Ha'amek Davar* that as a whole it does have certain similarities to verse. Most important is the fact that, like verse, the Torah contains a great deal of meaning that must be teased out from its terse wording. Moreover, the Torah was ideally meant to be memorized in its entirety.

them the song or to simply inform them of it. Rather, the expression connotes an unusual relationship between words and speaker.

Based on its usage elsewhere as well as on its literal meaning, the expression of placing words in someone's mouth connotes a strong dichotomy between the words and the speaker whose mouth eventually receives them. With regard to other places in the Bible where the expression is used, the most famous is with the prophecy of Bil'am. There, the gentile prophet makes it quite clear that it is not he who owns the prophetic words that he speaks, but rather that it is always God Who "puts them into [his] mouth."[4] Likewise earlier, Moshe is instructed to put his own words "into the mouth" of his spokesman, Aharon.[5]

The expression is similarly found in the Prophets with regard to the speech of the wise woman chosen by Yoav to help David and Avshalom resolve their differences.[6] There too, the woman's words clearly belong to someone else. Likewise concerning *Ha'azinu*: even if the speakers learn the song very well, somehow they will never own it. It will always remain foreign in a way that the *Shema* passages are not.[7] The reason for this will become evident as we further explore what characterizes this unusual section, placed close to the end of the Torah.

Ha'azinu is not completely *sui generis*. The Torah itself contains a handful of "songs" and the rest of the Tanach contains several more. Rather than implying music, these songs could best be described as lyrical poems. Still, even if music would not always accompany them, they were composed with sound and rhythm in mind. In fact, their rhythm is further accentuated by the distinctive fashion in which they are written on the traditional parchment scroll. There, each phrase is given its own aligned position, separated from the phrases both before and after it.

These sections are more easily memorized than the prose that surrounds

---

4   *Bemidbar* 23:12.

5   *Shemot* 4:15.

6   *II Shmuel* 14.

7   Granted, the *Shema* contains the instruction to place God's words on the hearts and souls of the Jews (*Devarim* 11:18). Still, the parallel is not complete and does not have the same connotation of making the words of the *Shema* foreign.

them, even as their artistic form makes them more difficult to understand. This is particularly important here, as memorization is explicitly one of *Ha'azinu's* main goals, something more or less exclusive to this song alone. It was apparently not enough merely to recite it regularly, reading it from a written text or repeating it after someone else. It had to be internalized to the point where every Jew would know it by heart.[8] And yet, in spite of all this, it was to retain the foreignness of something that is only "*placed* in our mouths." In *Ha'azinu's* unique combination of proximity and remoteness, it is literally under our skin and yet remains a foreign object.

A Dismal Reminder

Why did the *Ha'azinu* song need to remain somewhat foreign? One likely reason was its bitter message that the Jewish people would have certainly preferred to ignore. The metaphor of an unpleasant substance being placed into one's mouth is in contemporary terms reminiscent of bitter medicine that a child is forced to swallow. Like the child, the Jewish people surely did not want to hear that they would eventually fail in their loyalty to God and His Torah. Nor did they want to hear about the harsh punishments that would ensue. Yet, like medicine, it was to benefit the Jews, at the very least as a preventive, but also to reassure them that no matter how far they strayed, they would never be totally destroyed.

Ha'azinu's message to the Jewish people is rather primal in that it strips down God's relationship with them to the bottom line, which is that the Jews' betrayal of God will never bring its most logical conclusion – their obliteration. In this song, everything else is secondary. As opposed to the *bikkurim* declaration, here there is no need to mention the historical miracles God wrought for His people. In the *bikkurim* declaration, mention of the miracles was meant to engender gratitude. Here, however, gratitude is not sought. The gist is much more fundamental: that even though the Jews will act in such a way that *should* end the relationship, God will not allow it to end. Period.

8   See *Eruvin* 54b.

Nevertheless, while the Jews are assured of survival, *Ha'azinu* is a far cry from a romantic story of God's holding on to His beloved. Instead, it is a declaration that God's assured preservation of the Jewish people is the best thing that can be expected in such circumstances. It also hints to an endless loop: The reason given for God's decision not to destroy the Jews is that it would mislead others into thinking that they had the power to subdue His chosen nation.[9] If God were to destroy His nation, it had to be apparent that it was He Who destroyed them and not anyone else. But the only appropriate mechanism for doing this was to have other nations subdue them, which was itself intrinsically flawed for the reason just mentioned – that those nations would attribute it to their own power. Thus, problematic as the Jews might be, there was simply no way to discard them once they had been selected as God's representatives on earth.

This is hardly the stuff of national anthems,[10] nor is it typical Biblical fare. What nation would proudly proclaim their disloyalty to God, safe in the knowledge that He has to spare them only because His plans leave Him with no other choice? Although the Jews are often warned of terrible consequences if they betray God, the usual refrain is that after being punished they will learn their lesson and return to Him. Here, we don't see this, and instead read that He will *not destroy them completely*,[11] and that He will also eventually avenge their blood.[12] In *Ha'azinu*, the Torah wants to get this message across and no more.

What's the Point?

Given the dismal tone of the song, one wonders why the Jews had to remember it. And not only remember it, but memorize it as if it was of primary importance.

---

9   *Devarim* 32:27.
10   Malbim (*Devarim* 31:19) does in fact identify *Ha'azinu* as a type of national anthem. This makes sense given his unique understanding of the song's message (see below).
11   *Devarim* 32:26–27.
12   Ibid., verse 41.

Malbim presents a creative metaphor to answer this question:

> A king freed a slave from jail and appointed him in charge of the royal treasury. The king knew that this man had a long history of robbery, and in all likelihood would steal from the king, incurring his own death sentence. However, the king didn't want the man to die. And so he recorded the entire episode in his royal archive: that the man was an incurable thief and that the king himself appointed him as head of the treasury with full knowledge of his character. Anyone who read the entry in the royal records thought that the purpose of the record was to deter and warn the thief that if he stole he would be severely punished. But in truth, it was a reminder for the king himself to treat the thief lightly should he steal again. After all, the king had selected the thief with full knowledge.
>
> Similarly here; God says: I know that they will sin in the future, and therefore, "write down this song" for your own good. "Teach it to the children of Israel; memorize it," let it be in your memory, on the tips of your tongues, as an excuse, an explanation to Me so that you not be punished, "in order that this song be a testimony for Me regarding the children of Israel."[13]

According to Malbim, then, *Ha'azinu* wasn't meant for actual everyday *use*, even if it had to be recited all the time. The Torah says as much, prefacing the command given to Moshe to write and teach this song by the prognosis that the Jews will reach such a nadir of moral corruption that they won't even understand why punishments are coming to them.[14] It was at such a time that the song was meant to be employed.

Ha'azinu was meant to be ready in case of emergency, and like all emergency procedures, it wouldn't be useful if it weren't kept fresh. In that sense, the learning of this passage could be likened to a fire drill. So long as the Jews were living within the parameters of spiritual normalcy, there was no need to bring it out for anything but practice. It was only to be "used" when the Jews

---

13 Malbim, *Devarim* 31:19, translation based on that of R. Alex Israel.
14 *Devarim* 31:14–18.

had reached rock bottom and needed reassurance that they were not to face total annihilation. At that point, it would not be enough to merely calm them down and reassure them with regard to the consequences of sinning, but it *would* be enough to give them the assurance that all would not be lost and indeed would never be lost. That was the song's purpose.

God didn't need to be reminded. He knew His own will. But even as God would not destroy them, there would be times so dismal that the Jews were in danger of losing faith in, and destroying, themselves. *Ha'azinu* was meant to remind the Jews never to give up on themselves, in the same way that God would never give up on them.

It would be a bit far-fetched to say that the Jews would be able to use *Ha'azinu* as a sort of shield against God's anger, but their invoking it also reminded them that God's eternal choice came with Divine foresight. He knew that there would be times when things got so bad with the Jews that the only way to salvage His original plan would be to protect the Jews from His own attribute of justice, even though they had done nothing to deserve His mercy.

As Jews are fond of saying about such things, *nechama purta* – small comfort! But that is precisely why the song would not be invoked except under drastic circumstances. God warned Moshe that there would inevitably be such occasions on the long road to messianic times. The Jews needed to be ready to make use of the only consolation available during those terrible times. Small comfort perhaps, but it would be enough when nothing else was available.

Let us now return to the idea behind the song that would remain external to the Jewish people, even as they put it "into their mouths."

Marked by God

To understand *Ha'azinu*, we need Yeshayahu, the prophet known for some of the most daunting warnings ever given. Yeshayahu begins his book with a linguistically related rebuke, castigating the Jews as being worse than animals.[15]

---

15 *Yeshayahu* 1:1–9. The prophet is clearly referring back to *Ha'azinu* when he uses the same introductory words (in a different order) to introduce his song. As in *Ha'azinu*,

The crux of his speech is that since even an animal is loyal to its master, so too should the Jews be loyal to God. As with the song in *Ha'azinu*, Yeshayahu is discussing a very simple, even primal relationship. Moreover, here too, God is not looking for gratitude from the Jews. Rather, Yeshayahu plainly presents the fundamental tenet that the Jews belong to God, just like an animal belongs to its master.

While he doesn't speak about placing a song in the mouths of the Jews, Yeshayahu does bring up the relationship between men and their domesticated animals which sheds valuable light on why the words (and rhythm/music) of *Ha'azinu* needed to be placed "in the mouths" of the Jews.

The way to indicate ownership of an animal is by making a permanent mark on it – by branding it, for instance. Another way is to insert some sort of tag inside an accessible part of its body, like its ear or its mouth. I am not alluding to any specific practice that might have been well known in the Ancient Near East or even more generally. What I am suggesting is that the forceful placing of a mark or object on an animal is a classic way of denoting mastery over it, which is as true today as it was back then. I am also suggesting that forcing words into a person's mouth is also a way of showing ownership by the One Who (or one who) placed them there. Incidentally, such an allusion fits very well with the Bil'am story as well, where one finds a subtle parallel between Bil'am's nuanced mastery over his animal and God's much less nuanced mastery over Bil'am.

The idea that the placement of something foreign onto a person is meant to indicate primal ownership is further reinforced by the story of Kayin and Hevel. There God protects Kayin by placing a sign upon him.[16] We are not told what the sign is nor how it protects him from others, but the most straightforward meaning is that the sign is indicative of God's ownership and consequent

---

Yeshayahu uses the earth and sky as witnesses. He also invokes the comparison to Sedom and Amorrah and makes several other allusions to the song. As for his message, he says that in their state of spiritual dullness, the Jews of his time are even worse than animals, which at the very least understand that they have a vested interest in pleasing their masters.

16 *Bereshit* 4:15.

protection of Kayin and, accordingly, that anyone who attacks Kayin will risk running into trouble with God Himself.

We can conclude, then, that the *Ha'azinu* song not only serves to encourage the Jews in times of national emergency, it also serves as a marker denoting their permanent association with God. This is what gives them the safety hatch to begin with. For no matter how poorly they behave, they are literally "branded" as God's people.

* * *

Commitments rarely mean what they used to. The most obvious manifestation of this is the soaring rates of divorce around the world. And with trends toward globalization, commitment to one's nation is not what it used to be either. Patriotism and loyalty to one's country have almost become the abstract contractual obligation envisioned by the classical liberal philosophers instead of any sort of heartrending engagement to the homeland.

Of course, I am not saying that there is no place for casual friendships and acquaintances, but I do not believe that all relationships are meant to be casual. While we share a basic responsibility for everyone we meet, that is only a bare minimum. Family creates a deeper level of responsibility, as does community. This is formalized by halacha as well, wherein we see a hierarchy of whom to help when we are not able to help everybody.[17]

Our closest relationships should entail a deep, primal commitment. One will sometimes help his children for no other reason than the connection which exists between parent and child. For a child to grow up emotionally and spiritually healthy, he needs to know of that primal relationship, even though that is usually not the motivation behind the care he receives from his parents. His relationship with his parents is generally marked by love and pride on their part, which override attention to his less admirable qualities. But within the course of a lifetime, it is not uncommon for a child to act in such a way as to relinquish all but the primal bond between him and his parents.

What is true within the family is equally true within the nation. I am not suggesting that we engage in an ethic of "My country, right or wrong." Indeed,

17 See *Shulchan Aruch, Yoreh De'ah* 251.

God does not. He punishes the Jewish people, sometimes very severely. But what I am suggesting is that the essential relationship to one's people should never be severed. Moreover, as with *Ha'azinu*, everyone should make clear, not only to their nation but also to all those with whom they are essentially bonded, that things can get very bad, but that, regardless, the relationship will never die.

CHAPTER 9

Moshe's Blessings and the "New Order"

I N THE SAME way the blessings of Ya'akov provide a certain closure to the entire book of *Bereshit*,[1] so too, Moshe's blessings at the end of the book of *Devarim* provide similar resolution. And since their place is also the end of the entire Torah, they may carry even more significance.

Two questions are fundamental to a proper understanding of Moshe's final act: To what extent did Moshe feel a need to bless the Jewish people, and what was he trying to accomplish by doing so? Regarding the first question, one commentator goes so far as to suggest that it was an afterthought, only meant to reassure the Jewish people after the harsh rebuke he had just given them.[2] If, as several commentators understand it, the blessings are simply words of encouragement, such a suggestion could be plausible. Yet it is hard to leave it at that, as the many unusual features of this section compel us to look more closely. As we examine the structure and content of the blessings, what emerges is a strong case for saying that Moshe had much more than just encouragement in mind.

It is natural to compare and contrast Moshe's blessings with those of Ya'akov. The similarities are obvious: both foundational leaders[3] bless the twelve tribes right before they die. The differences are also easy to find: not only does Moshe change the order of the tribes to be blessed, he dramatically

---

1   *Redeeming Relevance in Exodus*, pp. 73–75.
2   Abarbanel, Introduction to *parashat Zot haBeracha*.
3   See *Redeeming Relevance in Exodus*, Chapter Three, especially pp. 47–50, for an analysis of the many similarities between the lives of these seminal leaders.

changes the content of almost all the blessings (the similarity between Yosef's two blessings is an exception, although it illustrates that Moshe could have chosen to echo most of Ya'akov's other blessings as well). The reason for any of these deviations is far from obvious, and the majority of commentators struggle to find the reason.

The order of the blessings is as follows:[4]

Ya'akov	Moshe
Reuven (Leah)	Reuven (Leah)
Shimon/Levi (Leah)	Yehudah (Leah)
Yehudah (Leah)	**Levi** (Leah)
Zevulun (Leah)	Binyamin (Rachel)
Yissachar (Leah)	**Yosef** (Rachel)
Dan (Bilhah)	Zevulun/Yissachar (Leah)
Gad (Zilpah)	Gad (Zilpah)
Asher (Zilpah)	Dan (Bilhah)
Naftali (Bilhah)	Naftali (Bilhah)
Yosef (Rachel)	Asher (Zilpah)
Binyamin (Rachel)	

We immediately note that Moshe blesses the more important tribes first and the less important tribes later. At the very least, this tells us that the order is not random. Moreover, Leah's more significant children (i.e., Reuven, Levi and Yehudah) come, as is always the case, before Rachel's children. Looking more carefully, we also see several deviations from the birth order of each subgroup, most prominently the listing of Yehudah before Levi, and Binyamin before Yosef. Also curious is the placement of Binyamin and Yosef in the middle of Leah's tribes, specifically between Levi and Zevulun. (Shimon is not mentioned at all, although many commentators understand him to be subsumed under Yehudah.[5])

---

4 Those receiving what we will call superblessings later in this chapter are bolded. Mothers' names are indicated, as this will also be of some significance.

5 See, for example, Ramban, *Devarim* 33:6–7.

R. Avraham Ibn Ezra is the first major commentator to try to make sense of the order and does an admirable job in finding reasons for the unexpected divergences from the birth (or any other obvious) order. Most important is his suggestion that Yehudah and Binyamin's future territorial proximity necessitates the proximity of their blessings. He adds that Levi is placed between them since that priestly tribe's center would be in Jerusalem, which lies between the other two tribes.[6] Many subsequent commentators adopt his general approach and summarize it as being based on the configuration of the *nachala*, the territorial inheritance, which also helps explain why Reuven is first (though his status as the firstborn means that there really isn't a great need for explanation vis-à-vis him to begin with).[7]

Moshe's Two Groupings

Ibn Ezra's line of reasoning, however, fails to explain one important fact: There is a long gap (*petucha*) only between the blessings of Yehudah and Levi,[8] whereas the Torah separates all the other blessings with a short gap (*setuma*) between each one. While most commentators pass over this curious deviation, there is one from the modern era, Netziv, who brings it to our attention.

Netziv suggests that the Torah is presenting two groups to us: Reuven and Yehudah on one side and the rest of the other tribes on the other. Of course, noticing this distinction is much simpler than explaining it. Netziv's explanation that the first two tribes operated on a more earthly, natural level (which he calls *malchut*, monarchy) whereas the latter operated on a more miraculous level of Divine intervention (which he calls *tiferet*, splendor) seems rather

6   Ibn Ezra, *Devarim* 33:6.

7   See, for example, Ramban, Rabbenu Bachya ben Asher, Abarbanel. Nevertheless, saying that it is based on the order of the tribes' geographic inheritance uncovers almost as many problems as it solves. It is for this reason that Abarbanel is forced to say that the explanation does not pertain to the last four tribes.

8   According to the Keter Aram Tzova text, the oldest and most reliable version of the Torah. It should be noted, however, that the Leningrad Codex does not have such a deviation, but rather shows the gap between these two blessings as the same as all of the others.

speculative.[9] Before returning to his approach, let us look for an explanation more grounded in the text.

One way to gain better insight into the separation of Reuven and Yehudah from the rest of the tribes is to focus on the most important differences between the blessings given by Moshe and those given by Ya'akov. Ya'akov distinguishes his two most illustrious sons, Yehudah and Yosef, by giving them what we could call "superblessings." Both in length and in quality, the blessings of these two brothers suggest special treatment. Given the leadership they had shown during Ya'akov's lifetime, it is understandable that he earmarks them to be at the forefront of the Jewish people in the future as well. Judging by future events, his blessings hit their mark, at least through most of the Biblical period, when the rivalry between the two brothers is embodied by the split of the tribes into the kingdoms of Yehudah and what is often referred to as Ephraim (Yosef's dominant son), or Yisrael. The special role these two brothers play extends even beyond the Biblical period, for even after the exile of Yosef's descendants, prophets still looked forward to the leadership of both Yosef and Yehudah in the messianic era.[10]

Moshe follows Ya'akov's general example in the bestowing of two superblessings, but gives it an interesting twist. Like Ya'akov, Moshe awards Yosef a superblessing, even repeating some key phrases from the former's blessing. But with regard to the second superblessing, Moshe boldly replaces Yehudah with Levi, his own tribe. Not only is the blessing transferred to Levi, its focus is changed as well. When Ya'akov gave Yehudah his blessing, the focus was clearly on power and might: Yehudah is compared to a lion who is feared by all and who will have his hand on the neck of his enemies. He is to be the master of the scepter and the staff.[11]

Not so with Levi. Although Moshe's blessing to him concludes with an allusion to the blows he can land his enemies, the focus is clearly somewhere else. At the center is Moshe's declaration that Levi will "teach Your statutes to

---

9   *Ha'amek Davar* 33:7–8. This distinction follows Netziv's theory concerning the two possible ways for the Jews to inherit the Land of Israel which were discussed in Chapter One.

10 *Yechezkel* 37:16–17.

11 *Bereshit* 49:8–10.

Ya'akov and Your laws to Israel" on the one hand, and "place the incense before You and the sacrifice on Your altar" on the other.[12]

The significance of Moshe's move is rarely discussed but should not be underestimated. For one, the ideals that Moshe's transfer and transformation of the superblessing implies clearly impacts on the balance of power among the tribes: All of a sudden a new tribe is thrust into leadership, seemingly at the expense of Yehudah, the traditional front-runner for political power.

This change also mirrors a certain transformation that had already taken place on the Jewish people's way from Egypt to the Land of Israel. The Levite children of Amram – Moshe, Aharon and Miriam, had become the leaders of the Jewish people *de facto*. Beyond these three eminent personalities, the tribe of Levi had been promoted more generally via its new responsibility concerning the sacrificial rite and its trappings. Yet this did not mean the Levites had permanently displaced the tribes of Yosef and Yehudah. Even while the Jews were still in the desert, the tribal leaders who made a difference are from Yosef (Yehoshua, from the tribe of Ephraim) and Yehudah (Calev).

But if Yehudah would not lose its position of leadership, this doesn't mean that Moshe had to endorse it. We have already seen from Chapter One that Moshe was a man of vision; he was willing to propose lofty ideals that the Jewish people were not always able to attain. Thus, it appears that rather than confirming the current status quo, Moshe used the blessings as an attempt to create (or at least, model) a new sociopolitical order.

Moshe knew Yehudah would likely be the leader of any long-term monarchy created by the Jews. He also knew that such a monarchy would represent a triumph of mundane worldliness, wherein the exigencies of state would often derail the nation's spiritual agenda.[13] Such a system is certainly not what Moshe had in mind. Instead, he sought a state dominated by a spiritual leadership that would tower over a weak administrative arm, the latter meant only to keep the running of more practical matters under control. He certainly did not look forward to the creation of the complex infrastructure and political

---

12 *Devarim* 33:8–11.
13 See Chapter Seven.

glory that would eventually take form under David and Shlomo. Rather, his model of leadership was based on what he had largely created in his own day.

Under the very unusual circumstances of the desert, Moshe had become the undisputed leader whose clear focus was on the spiritual. This is very much in line with the blessing he gives to Levi, where leadership is not defined by domination of the other tribes and military prowess, but rather by mastery in the fields of education, law and worship.

Clearly, Levi would still need a "prime minister" to run the temporal affairs of state; that is precisely why Yehoshua's tribe of Yosef is given a superblessing. Yet it is clear that in "Moshe's state," Levi would set the tone. Moreover, to make sure that we know the subordinate place of Yosef in such an arrangement, his younger brother Binyamin is placed before him. (Not necessarily the only reason for this placement, but perhaps the most important one.)

This was also reflected in Moshe's desert administration. There, he was assisted in the more basic administration of the nation by his Ephraimite disciple and eventual successor, Yehoshua. In the desert as well as in Moshe's ideal Jewish state, we see a political leader who is to the religious leader what the moon is to the sun.[14] It gives off light when the sun is not visible. But even then, it never emits anything that is not a reflection of the sun itself.

In line with this ideal, Moshe also uses his blessings to try to limit Yehudah's more temporal sphere of influence to Reuven alone. Following Netziv's observation, we see Moshe wanting to create a sharp distinction between this tiny subgroup and the rest of the tribes that would now have Levi at the top. If Yehudah's influence could be contained, Levi could more easily dominate the rest of the tribes.

The New Order and the Old Order

What still needs explanation is why Moshe gives Yehudah a sphere of influence at all, and even more to the point why it includes specifically Reuven (and possibly Shimon). Most helpful here is to think of Moshe's division of

14 See *Bava Batra* 75a.

the tribes as that of a "New Order" and an "Old Order." His proposed arrangement was completely different from the arrangement up until this point. It required a new way of thinking, the kind of which is usually the most difficult for those ensconced in the power structures of the past.

The old power structures had been dominated by the four tribes that were descended from Leah's first group of children: Reuven, Shimon, Levi and Yehudah. Of these four, Levi would be not only the proponent of the New Order but also the tribe that had the most to gain from it. Taking Levi out, then, leaves us with a "new Old Order": Reuven, Shimon and Yehudah – precisely the tribes that Moshe put to one side.

It makes sense that Reuven is listed first in this new manifestation of the Old Order, even though Yehudah is the leader of the group. A hallmark trait of Old Orders in general, and of this one in particular, is loyalty to traditional authority, often embodied by birth order. Only in Levi's New Order can a younger brother precede his older brother, as was the case with Binyamin and Yosef there.

Placing Reuven with Yehudah may not have been only because both would support the Old Order against Levi's new one. First of all, Reuven is characterized by problematic idiosyncrasies. Between the jealousy shown toward Levi by the Reuveni leaders Datan and Aviram on the one hand, and the tribe's preference to stay in Transjordan on the other, Moshe might have seen them as a particularly troublesome group.[15] Consequently, it was wiser to leave them out of the more refined state of affairs that Moshe wanted to create. Furthermore, Moshe may have foreseen that their recalcitrant character would be best suited to the sharp discipline of a Yehudah state. And if Moshe also included Shimon in this grouping, much of the same could be said of this tribe, if not necessarily for the same reasons.[16]

---

15   See *Redeeming Relevance in Numbers*, Chapter Five.
16   Ibid., Chapter Seven.

The Other Jewish State

But what would be the fate of Yehudah's sphere of influence according to Moshe? Obviously, Moshe didn't want its complete destruction. If that were the case, Reuven and Yehudah would have been omitted from the blessings altogether – as was the case with their brother Shimon. And if that were too radical, Moshe could have advocated for the complete dissolution of the old order by putting Reuven and Yehudah after Levi and perhaps even after Binyamin and Yosef. So if, as it appears, Yehudah's leadership role was not slated for demise, what did Moshe want from this tribe?

Instead of Yehudah having a specific job to perform concurrently with those of Levi and Yosef, Moshe may have seen Yehudah taking the role of an alternative type of leader when the situation called for it. The Old Order tribes would represent a fallback leadership model, to be brought out when the Jews would fail to live up to the higher standards of the New Order. Moshe's vision of the future of Jewish leadership is thus similar to Netziv's two-tiered approach concerning Jewish leadership in the desert.[17] As discussed in Chapter One, the ideal situation of immediate and intense Divine presence reflected in the desert experience would be fraught with danger if the Jews could not live according to its required discipline. It was therefore important for there to be a contingency plan which would require less discipline, even if it came at the expense of the Jews losing the intensity of God's involvement with them. While the great cost incurred by moving to such a leadership model is self-evident, once needed, the only alternative to it would have been total obliteration of the Jewish people.

Although his comments are not directly connected to the blessings, Netziv suggests that Moshe acquiesced to a lower-level fallback position in the desert.[18] This would certainly indicate that Moshe was aware of the usefulness of such an idea. Hence even if he wanted the Israelites to now move back to the higher level experienced immediately after leaving Egypt, he likely intuited

---

17 See note 9.

18 Earlier (p. 31) we contested Netziv on this point. Nevertheless, his idea serves as a helpful paradigm to explain Moshe's thinking regarding the future.

that they would still need a contingency plan. The tribes of the Old Order not only represented this, it was their responsibility to keep it alive.

Indeed, the contingency plan was put into use over and over. For one, the monarchy of Yehudah, established by David, can certainly be seen as a withdrawal from the New Order ideal. This is why, when the Jews claim the need for a monarchy, God declares it to be a rejection of Him more than anything else.[19] Obviously, if it were a complete rejection, lacking nuance, it is hard to imagine that God would have acquiesced. Presumably then, what the Jewish people were actually requesting was a lower level of Divine intervention. This would mean they would no longer be harassed by their neighbors each time they failed to keep God's commandments, but it would also mean that they would be relinquishing overt Divine protection from the normal political and military ambitions of other nations. This, in turn, would create the need for a more centralized government that could put together an army worthy of the name. And this is exactly what served as the focus of their request.

This is how things would be until the messianic period, when the temporal leader will also be the spiritual leader. Given the tradition that the messianic king will come from the house of David, and consequently from the tribe of Yehudah, the political vision that Moshe identified with Levi will at the end of days finally be adopted by Yehudah as well.

The Need for Dreams

Moshe's vision for a New Order could easily be discounted as one more tragic failure of a leader who set his sights too high. It is obvious that the blessings, as we have portrayed them, had little effect on the Jews after they conquered the Land of Israel. Nor is it clear whether the blessings had any impact even during the early period, when the Jews first entered the land. Granted, the tenure and especially the conquests of Yehoshua do carry a shadow of Moshe's vision, characterized as they were by so much Divine intervention. There one captures a glimpse of Yosef's descendant in charge of a temporal conquest but

19   *I Shmuel* 8:7. See also Chapter Five.

still deeply rooted in a spiritual quest. Yet Yehoshua acts only as a reflection of the light of his departed teacher – a teacher he did not truly replace. Instead, there arose a vacuum of spiritual leadership which, once Yehoshua died, led to a cycle of sin and failure. And once the judges are replaced by Yehudah's monarchy, Moshe's vision gradually fades from the scene altogether.

Yet this is not the only way to look at what transpired when the Jews entered and settled their land. Visions are much more than just plans meant to be followed. They are at least as much about an ideal as they are about a prescription for the future. As such, the success of a vision need not depend on whether or not it materializes.

As an ideal, Moshe's vision is meant to provide the answer when Jews are asked, "What do you *really* want?" If the Jews have rarely attempted to attain what Moshe let us know we should "really want," it is far from a rejection of his ideal. Rather, it is an admission that we are not there yet.

Moshe's blessings represent a concretized way to transmit a national vision. They are a spiritual legacy that his nation has since always known to be its ideal. Traditional Jews are meant to hope for the attainment of that ideal sooner rather than later. Yet when we are pursuing a spiritual journey, we know that we can't be certain of when we will get there, or even whether we will get there at all. Be that as it may, our journey is forever informed and illuminated by the proverbial light that Moshe shone for us at the end of the tunnel.

* * *

It is surprising how many people cannot verbalize what it is they really want. It is even more surprising how many people have not even asked themselves this question, let alone tried to answer it.

We live in more pragmatic times, where we are bidden to seek realistic goals. There is something to be said for that, yet it should not come at the expense of dispensing with lofty goals and ideals. In fact, the loftier the better. For it to serve its purpose, a true ideal must inspire. And to do that, it must never be based on an underestimation of our tremendous potential.

Great visions are the products of great people. If there is a lack of vision today, it reflects a sore absence of people of true stature. One way to engender greatness, however, is to remind ourselves of the greatest and, consequently, the least practical visions of the past – visions such as Moshe's that were almost doomed from the start. For it is precisely because they are so far out of reach that they are so inspiring. And if a vision is not inspiring, it is, by definition, a failure. In the end, then, the failure of Moshe's vision is not only a tribute to its greatness. It is also a tribute to its actual success.

CHAPTER 10

The Death of Moshe

I N *Redeeming Relevance in the Book of Exodus*, we mentioned that Moshe's personality is larger than life.[1] As a rule, we come to understand the figures of the Bible by comparing and contrasting them with one another, and even with ourselves. But, to whom can Moshe be compared? In his death as well as in his life he defies comparison.

It is not surprising that the Torah's handling of Moshe's death is unique, bolstering our impression that he's in a league of his own. All other outstanding figures receive only summary statements from the Biblical narrative when they die. By contrast, Moshe is singled out with the type of praise that could best be described as a eulogy. Surely we are meant to pause and reflect on this great individual, all the more so as it comes right at the end of the Torah. We might be tempted to find a parallel in the death of Ya'akov, which also comes at a conceptual and literary point of transition, near the end of the book of *Bereshit*. Yet not only is there no eulogy for Ya'akov, the Torah seems to go out of its way to make sure that his death is not at the very end of *Bereshit*. Instead, it is followed by stories of his sons' continued lives in Egypt, presumably showing that life does not end with the death of this great and final patriarch.

The praise given to Moshe is only one side of the unusual treatment he receives. The Torah also presents less complementary details – for example, that his death comes as a result of his sin – which seem clearly aimed at curbing our enthusiasm. It is as if the Torah's presentation of Moshe's death represents

---

1   p. 37.

a balancing act, letting us know how great he was without allowing us get carried away and lose our sense of perspective. Why was that needed only with Moshe?

There is a great deal at stake with Moshe's death. The Torah's authority and reliability largely revolve around the status of his prophecy.[2] The ambivalence felt in the treatment of his death is more than just a question of editorial balance, then. On the one hand, given the weight Jewish tradition places on the authority of Moshe's prophecy, there is an important need to discourage challenges to it. In order to do so, the Torah, at this very important point in Moshe's story, must make his special understanding of God's will quite clear. To accomplish this, his obvious mortality must be tempered by an almost superhuman description of who he actually was. On the other hand, making too strong a statement about Moshe's greatness could lead to worshiping him instead of God.

Thus the Torah goes back and forth, first pointing out Moshe's sin and reminding us that he is duly chastised – just like any other mortal not meeting the expectations of God; and then telling us of his superlative abilities and accomplishments. The back and forth that will characterize this section is the key to the paradox that Moshe represents, both in the Torah and in Jewish tradition more broadly: He has to be eminently human and relatable to all the rest of us, yet so great as to defy comparison.

Brothers in Life and in Death

If we have already seen the difficulties in comparing Moshe's and Ya'akov's deaths, we can look elsewhere for parallels to Moshe's death. Perhaps it should be expected that Moshe's manner of leaving the world would be most similar to the way Aharon, his brother, left it. To begin with, both brothers die in exile as a result of their failures in the desert.[3] As Moshe's death approaches,

---

2   See *Mishneh Torah, Hilchot Yesodei haTorah* 8.

3   Though not immediately relevant, it is interesting in this context to note the parallels between Moshe and Aharon's deaths on the one hand, and Miriam's death on the other. The most obvious parallel is her burial outside the Land of Israel. But here

the Torah emphasizes that he will not be allowed to go over the Jordan, first spelling out his failure to sanctify God when bringing forth water from the boulder[4] and later alluding to it.[5] Such a description clearly echoes Aharon's demise, which is also attributed to his sin at Mei Merivah.[6] In Aharon's case, however, the Torah sees no need to summarize his life, instead merely describing his death and the children of Israel's mourning for him.

Besides mention of their common sin, the two brothers' deaths are also characterized by their unusual mountaintop locations. In Moshe's case, it may partly be in order for him to see the Land of Israel before he dies. Moreover, if he could not be buried in the land that he loved, perhaps a mountaintop overlooking it would be the next best thing. Yet the fact that Aharon also dies on a mountaintop – presumably nowhere near the Land of Israel – leads us to believe that being buried on a mountain has other significance as well.

In the Bible as in common parlance, height is often associated with God.[7] Thus, it is no coincidence that the two most important locations of revelation, Mount Sinai and Mount Moriah (the site of the Temple in Jerusalem) are mountaintops. Indeed, most people are familiar with the well-known Midrash concerning which mountain was the most fit to host the giving of the Torah.[8] That the Midrash does not include a valley or plateau to vie for the honor reflects the association of topographical elevation with holiness.

Hence the simplest explanation for the brothers' burials on mountaintops is to stress their spiritual elevation. Both of them dedicated their lives to impressing the will of God on the Jewish people – and on some level, on mankind as a whole. Moshe was the one to receive direct prophecy from God, and

---

we are somewhat perplexed, as there is no indication of her being involved in a sin that merits what is repeatedly described as a punishment for Moshe and Aharon. See the conclusions at the end of this section, which could apply not only to Aharon but to Miriam as well.

4   *Devarim* 32:51.

5   Ibid., 34:4.

6   *Bemidbar* 20:24.

7   See, for example, *Bereshit* 14:20, 22 and *Tehillim* 138:6, where God is described as being high or lofty. See also *Sukkah* 4b, which, based on *Shemot* 25:22, discusses how God does not descend to the ground but stays above it.

8   *Bemidbar Rabba* 13:3.

God's investiture of Aharon as his brother's mouthpiece became a permanent feature of the Torah's transmission in the desert.[9]

Granted, Aharon is not generally viewed as holier than other Biblical heroes who were not buried on mountains. Yet, since his being buried outside the Land of Israel may lead one to the opposite conclusion – that he was less holy – there was a need to remind us of his holiness. God, therefore, had him buried on a "high" place.

Aharon's unique burial place can also be explained from a different perspective. In the same way that his sin can be attributed merely to association with his brother,[10] so too might be his greatness. The two brothers (and perhaps their sister as well[11]) are a team, such that many of the honors bestowed on Moshe – as well as his punishment – are likewise bestowed upon the rest of the group.

The identification of the two brothers as a team that earns the same rewards is also played out in their unique, thirty-day mourning period.[12] This period of mourning is quite familiar to observant Jews, although the Bible mentions it only with regard to Moshe and Aharon. More specifically, the Torah's unique reference to the mourning period, and its description with regard to both Moshe and Aharon as a time for crying, shows the intimate bond between the generation of the desert and their two leaders.

The people cried for this length of time because Moshe and Aharon were as much this generation's parents as they were its leaders. But they were not only bound to the desert generation, they were also bound to their task. Given that they were barred entry into the land, it would be all too easy to forget their huge accomplishment of taking a large, nomadic clan and turning it into

9   *Shemot* 4:14–16.

10   See *Sifrei, Devarim* 33:8, which alludes to this and which is cited with even more emphasis by Rashi on the same verse. See also *Ha'amek Davar, Bemidbar* 20:24, 27, who endeavors to identify Aharon's sin, ultimately concluding that it was mostly associated with the actions of his younger brother.

11   See note 1.

12   While the Torah mentions seventy days of crying and mourning at the death of Ya'akov, this is attributed to all of Egypt and not specifically to his family, whereas we only read about his family mourning for seven days after his burial. See *Bereshit* 50:1–11.

a nation that would serve as God's vanguard on earth. Although they were not allowed to see their mission all the way through, the Torah wants us to be aware of the great honor due them for their efforts.

Separated in Life and in Death

Beyond the parallels between the two brothers' deaths and their rewards (and punishments), in the case of Moshe, the uniqueness of his death goes far beyond Aharon's. As unusual as Aharon's death was, it was not nearly as unusual as the death of Moshe. The Torah needs to emphasize Moshe's lofty status, and consequently offers us a great deal of information not otherwise found in a Biblical death narrative. Most important among these details is what we described above as a eulogy. But not only is the Torah's extolling Moshe at his death unusual, how it does so is unique as well.

The superlative quality of Moshe's praise here is well worth our notice. As if it were not clear enough, the Torah uses the word *kol* ("all") six times in the last two verses of Moshe's eulogy (which are also the last two verses of the Torah). Furthermore, to completely crystallize its point, the Torah emphatically states that "there never again arose a prophet . . . like Moshe."[13] This description would be further refined in Jewish theology through the years,[14] but the Torah is the first to emphasize that Moshe is in a category uniquely his own.

Of almost equal importance as the unique praise given Moshe's lifework is the clause informing us that all his feats were done "in the eyes of all of Israel." Here the Torah is telling us that the critical acknowledgment of Moshe's stature is significantly enhanced by the *public* knowledge of it. The Torah uses this as its concluding statement, establishing for all time that what made Moshe unique was known to the entire Jewish people and was not just an esoteric secret revealed only to a privileged few.

Another unique feature of Moshe's death is his anonymous burial place.

13 *Devarim* 34:10.
14 See *Mishneh Torah, Hilchot Yesodei haTorah* 7:6.

Abarbanel takes this one step further and suggests that there was actually no burial altogether. Rather, he posits, Moshe's body simply returned to its basic elements, without having to first decompose. But even without going that far, an anonymous burial place that would never be visited is unusual enough. Moreover, the Torah makes a point of mentioning that the burial place was not known later either.[15]

Many claim that the anonymity of this grave was intended to prevent it from becoming an object of worship.[16] Given the subsequent treatment of other gravesites at different points in history, this was no negligible danger. But as with most things, there are different ways to accomplish the same goal. God could have simply put Moshe's grave in a place that could not be reached, such as in the depths of the sea. Alternatively, He could have had Moshe simply rise into the sky like the prophet Eliyahu – though such a suggestion is problematic in its own right, as we will soon discuss. Hence it appears that there was something particularly fitting about concealing Moshe's tomb.

The key to Moshe's burial lies in the manner in which he lived his life. In Moshe's case – although not only in his case – being unique also meant being lonely. This was central to his singular role as the intermediary between God and the Jewish people.[17] And it makes sense that what was imperative in life would also be necessary in death.

Moshe had a family, yet his connection to his wife and children was more a formality than anything else. This is brought indelibly home by his solitary final scene. His role required him to live alone and to die alone.[18]

We read that he died "by the mouth of God" and that "he/He buried him." While some claim that Moshe buried himself,[19] the more obvious reading of this is that God buried him.[20] In either case, it is clear that Moshe died alone with God, in marked distinction to Aharon, who dies in the presence of his

---

15 *Devarim* 34:6.
16 See, for example, Rabbi S.R. Hirsch and Rabbi Y.S. Reggio, ibid.
17 *Redeeming Relevance in Exodus*, Chapter Three.
18 See *Ha'amek Davar, Devarim* 34:6.
19 This position is first advanced in *Sota* 14a and cited by Rashi in *Devarim* 34:6.
20 Rashi brings this position as well, ascribing it to Rabbi Yishmael.

brother and his oldest living son and successor, Elazar. It is also in contrast to almost everyone else mentioned in Tanach.[21]

It is not enough for Moshe to die by himself; his separation from family and nation must be total, even after his death. This too takes us back to *Redeeming Relevance in Exodus*,[22] where we suggest that since the Torah's message was partially directed to all the nations of the world, there was a need for its transmitter to transcend his origins and natural allegiance to the Jewish people. The universal facet of Moshe's identity was so central that it would need to be perpetuated. Thus, one of the major reasons his burial plot is forever hidden from the eyes of his people is because separation from them needed to be permanently enshrined. While it would be painful for the Jewish nation to part from Moshe forever, Jews throughout the generations would need to know that he was not entirely of their nation.

Moshe and Eliyahu

Besides Aharon, there is another Biblical hero whose death is comparable to that of Moshe: the prophet Eliyahu, who flies to Heaven in a fiery chariot. Both he and Moshe go upward, which as mentioned above signifies holiness. Both also, for all intents and purposes, disappear, Eliyahu leaving the earth and Moshe in the earth but inaccessible.

It makes sense that these two prophets' deaths resemble each other, as there are many other parallels between Moshe's and Eliyahu's respective careers. More than anything else, they were both of almost mythical stature, not quite of this world.[23] The commonalities in their deaths are ultimately a reflection of what they shared in their lives.

---

21 Chanoch (*Bereshit* 5:24) and Eliyahu (*II Melachim* 2:11), whom we will discuss below, might be in this category of dying alone with God. In any event, no one besides Moshe alone is buried by God.

22 *Redeeming Relevance in Exodus*, op. cit.

23 See the long list of parallels in *Pesikta Rabbati* 4 and its treatment in "Eliyahu uMoshe," in R. Yigal Ariel, *Mishpat Melucha* (Hispin: Midreshet haGolan, 1994), pp. 453–456.

One commentator asks why Moshe doesn't fly into the sky as well. After all, he says, isn't it even more fitting for Moshe to merit such a grand finale, which would show his favor with God once and for all?[24] While this might sound like a strong question, it neglects to take into consideration the other side of the Torah's balancing act. It is indeed important to show Moshe's elevated status, but not at the expense of causing people to turn him into a god. For someone of Moshe's unique stature – even more than for Eliyahu – not to have died like a mortal would likely have caused too many Israelites to elevate him to divine status.

Moshe the Mortal

The other side of the Torah's balancing act with Moshe requires our attention as well. We have already mentioned the importance of recounting Moshe's sin with the boulder at this point. Reminding us that Moshe sinned is a powerful way to reemphasize that Moshe is neither God nor an angel, neither of whom sin. That is clear enough. But merely recounting his sin is not sufficient in order to finally put the matter of his humanity to rest. Moshe needs to die the type of death common to all men, as far removed as possible from an otherworldly death such as, for instance, soaring into the skies in a fiery chariot.

Moshe's very human death is still not enough to fully emphasize his humanity, and his unique greatness must be put into context. For example, he is the first person ever to be called "a man of God,"[25] and is later given a fairly rare and in this case final accolade as a servant (or slave) of God.[26] Another honor is meriting a death by the word (literally, by the mouth) of God.[27] All of these praises are defined in terms of Moshe's close relationship with God, with emphasis on his subservient position in the face of the Divine.

Only God's dictates what Moshe will do, even when it comes time for him

---

24 I have not been able to locate the source of this opinion.

25 *Devarim* 33:1.

26 Ibid., 34:5. See *Sifrei* ad loc.; Nechama Leibowitz, *Studies in Devarim* (Jerusalem: World Zionist Organization, 1980), pp. 370–371.

27 *Devarim* 34:5.

to die. Indeed, before his death scene, Moshe is given what appears to be a command to die.[28] This puzzles some commentators. For short of committing suicide, which does not appear to be the intention, how does one decide to die? In view of our analysis, the command is given more to make a point to the reader than anything else: No matter how great Moshe is, he remains "like clay in the hands of the Potter."

Another curious feature that serves to make a similar point is when "the children of Israel cried for Moshe . . . thirty days, and [then] the days of the crying of mourning for Moshe ceased."[29] Compare this to the mourning for Aharon: "And the entire house of Israel cried for Aharon thirty days."[30] This is more natural, both conceptually and grammatically, since giving a specific time frame also informs us when the time period ends. To tell us that the days of mourning for Moshe stopped when they ended is superfluous.

What the Torah is doing here is stressing that life continued after Moshe died.[31] The Israelites were very sad, but they survived and continued with their lives once the mourning period ended. The Torah reinforces this notion further by mentioning Moshe's successor, Yehoshua, right before it begins eulogizing Moshe. Here too, the Torah wants to make sure we understand that life does not end with Moshe. Irreplaceable yes, but with no other choice, he is replaced nevertheless.

* * *

Moshe sets the limits on human achievement, and so the Torah confirms that there would be none like him. By looking at Moshe we see what is possible for a man to accomplish, and at the same time we see that the proverbial sky really is the limit. Being human creates boundaries, even for someone like Moshe,

---

28 Ibid., 32:50.

29 Ibid., 34:8.

30 *Bemidbar* 20:29.

31 Earlier, I suggested that the Torah shows us that life goes on after the death of Ya'akov by not having the book of *Bereshit* end with his death. While I am now arguing that the Torah wants to make the same point about Moshe's death, we must keep in mind the balancing act I have stressed. In the case of Moshe, the Torah had to end with Moshe's eulogy specifically in order to maintain the balance between Moshe's greatness and the fact that life would continue without him.

and he can do no more than follow the normal human life cycle: marry, have children, grow old and, eventually, die. But the temporal limits that death places in front of Moshe, and therefore in front of us as well, are not the only limits he faces. Like other humans, Moshe encounters spatial limits as well. He has a body and so can be in only one place at a time. His body being outside the Land of Israel axiomatically means that he would not be in the Land of Israel, in a way that would be meaningless when speaking about God. For when God was with Moshe at his burial site, He was also in the Holy Land and everywhere else as well. Not so Moshe – or any of us, for that matter.

Our limits are precisely what make us human. Both in time and in space, we can only stretch as far as our bodies will take us, and no more. For most of us this is all too obvious, and we make no claims to immortality. Yet for others, some of whom are able to accomplish great things, internalizing this is *the* challenge. The Torah's insistence on emphasizing Moshe's mortality is a response to these people and their admirers.

Moshe lived a life that was meant to get this very point across. His signature personality trait is identified in another section of the Torah as *"the man Moshe was more humble than any man."*[32] It is specifically because he was also superior to any man that this takes on such great significance. How should we understand this?

Most of us rarely examine our perspective on time and space – we think ten years is a long time and ten minutes is a short time. Likewise, we think of a mouse as a small animal and an elephant as a large one. That is all fine and well. The problem, however, is that we take this to be a *universally* true perspective. Yet if we were to think more carefully, we would realize that from an ant's perspective a mouse is really quite large and from a whale's perspective an elephant is not so impressive. Understanding that the human perspective is relative allows us greater insight into Moshe's success as a prophet. As Moshe grew to have a greater understanding of God, he most likely started looking at the world from *God's* perspective. And from that point of view, a man is very small indeed.

32 *Bemidbar* 12:3.

It is generally assumed that Moshe knew he was the greatest man to ever live. What enabled him to know this and still be extremely modest was his perspective. Compared to other humans, a great person might think very highly of himself. If, however, he sees himself from the perspective of God, he will feel quite humbled. To put if differently, even if you are the greatest ant in the world, how great can an ant be? Man's being far superior to an ant on many different levels notwithstanding, it would be difficult to claim that the difference between an ant and a man is greater than the difference between man and God.

It now makes sense that the greatest man was also the most humble. True humility comes from an elevated and ultimately *truer* perspective. As we end the Torah's last book, and with it the Torah, we can see both the greatness and the smallness of man in one complex bundle. Even more significant, however, is the knowledge that more than anything else, realizing our own smallness is what can make us truly great.